YACHTING
MONTHLY

Confessi

YACHTING
MONTHLY

Confessions

Yachtsmen own up to their sailing sins

Edited by Paul Gelder

Cartoons by Mike Peyton

ADLARD COLES NAUTICAL
London

Contents

Yachting Monthly Confessions

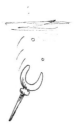

Adlard Coles Nautical
Bloomsbury Publishing Plc
50 Bedford Square, London WC1B 3DP
29 Earlsfort Terrace, Dublin 2, Ireland

ADLARD COLES NAUTICAL, ADLARD COLES and the Buoy logo are
trademarks of Bloomsbury Publishing Plc

First edition published 2000
Reprinted 2002, 2006, 2008
Reissued 2009
Reprinted 2011, 2012, 2014, 2015, 2016, 2018, 2019, 2020, 2021

ISBN 978-1-4081-1639-5

A CIP catalogue record for this book is available from the British Library.

Bloomsbury Publishing Plc makes every effort to ensure that the paper
used in the manufacture of our books are natural, recyclable products made
from wood grown in well-managed forests. Our manufacturing processes
conform to the environmental regulations of the country of origin.

18 20 19 17

Typeset in 10 1/2 / 13 1/2 Garamond Book
Printed and bound in Great Britain by CPI Group (UK) Ltd, Croydon CR0 4YY

Note: while all reasonable care has been taken in the publication
of this book, the publisher takes noresponsibility for the use
of the methods or products described in the book.

Preface

I MUST CONFESS
Yachting Monthly readers include policemen, princes, nurses, chefs, judges, priests and postmen. They drive trains, produce films and offer bank loans. In addition to boats, their interests range from agriculture to archaeology. They share the common denominators of sailing and a wry sense of humour.

An editor's job is to find out who and what they are and what moves them. Club bar encounters and scads of letters made me suspect a shared urge to confess their maritime sins—a process rich with possibilities for artistic interpretation.

I recalled the kindly old Irish priest of my childhood and the dusty darkness of the confessional: 'Ye've done none of dem tings my son,' he would sigh. 'Away wid ye and say tree Hail Marys.'

So I donned my biretta and waited. The response from readers was instant and gratifying. Readers beat their breasts with enthusiasm and confessed with total abandon.

Only pompous humbugs who are never wrong eschew the Confessional. They crawl dripping from their latest cock-ups, blaming everybody from the ship's cat upwards and everything from magnetic anomoly to potted shrimps. The Confessional is one of *Yachting Monthly*'s much-loved fixtures. If ever it is axed it will be when readers stop confessing—and pigs fly.

DES SLEIGHTHOLME
EDITOR OF *YACHTING MONTHLY* FROM 1967-1984

Mike Peyton

For many years the much sought after prize for those brave
enough to publicly confess their sailing sin was an original
Peyton cartoon. Mike Peyton, a writer as well as cartoonist, is
sometimes known as the Giles of the sailing scene. His keen eye
for humour afloat has inspired 17 books of cartoons and some
2000 Confessional cartoons.

Mike has owned 13 boats, from a Folkboat to a Dutch botter,
and three ferrocement boats, *Brimstone, Lodestone* and (his
latest) *Touchstone*, a 38ft ketch. There is no truth to the rumour
that his next boat will be called *Tombstone*.

Mike's cartoons have been published in sailing magazines from
Yokohama to Yarmouth. He lives on the East Coast in Fambridge,
on the River Crouch, and still draws the cartoon for the best
Confession each month in *Yachting Monthly*.

PAUL GELDER
DEPUTY EDITOR

Confessions

A night encounter

About eight nights out from Falmouth, heading towards San
Miguel during the 1979 Azores and Back race, my father and I
were becoming disenchanted with drifting around at less than
one knot and very much in need of reassurance that we were
not the last boat in the race nor indeed the only boat in the
world. What a night: no moon, more stars than you could
believe; it would have been superb if only we had been moving
faster.

'Look at that!' said my father, pointing to a bright light very
low on the horizon and so clear that you felt you could reach out
and touch it.

'It must be a white navigation light on another boat', I said.
'But it must be very close.'

We were so uplifted by the thought of another boat nearby
that we started blowing our foghorn and making as much noise
as possible in order to attract the attention of the people on
board.

After several minutes of shouting and blowing, we decided
that the light had to be a masthead light as we were now looking
up towards it. Strangely, though, we could see nothing of the boat
itself and we reckoned we had to be less than 100 yards apart. We
seemed to be getting nearer all the time, judging by the elevation
of the light, but never quite catching up.

You have all heard of people having mental problems during long voyages; you have probably all heard of dogs that bark at the moon...This is the first time I have ever admitted that I spent a small part of my life shouting and blowing a foghorn at Venus.
• *Bernard Kerrison*

Simple sail handling

Being married to an ardent, if inexperienced sailing enthusiast, for the past year I have tried to overcome my fear and taken to the water in our 25ft Westerly Tiger.

Many a wonderful day, I admit, I have spent bobbing about the Solent enjoying the scenery, the sun and the light winds. If this be sailing, I'm converted!

On one particular balmy day, I had taken the helm while my husband was, it seemed to me, fussing about with the sails: first sheeting in and then easing out, tightening this, loosening that, looking to the sky and then down to the sea. Why doesn't he go and do something useful, I thought, like put the kettle on.

Suddenly I saw a look of consternation in his face, for astern and gradually creeping up on us was another Westerly Tiger displaying its cruising chute in magnificent glory. In no time at all it had caught us up, and then, to my husband's horror, overtaken us. I knew he was going to suggest that we set a similar sail.

'Have you ever put this sail up before?' I asked rather nervously; I couldn't help noticing the way he was looking at the other boat and mentally taking notes. In what seemed a trice, the sail went up, the wind billowing it out—I was impressed!

'Sheet in, sheet in, S-h-e-e-t in!' he yelled, 'NOW!'

Too late, the sail was becoming well and truly wrapped, like an hour-glass, around the forestay. 'Oh my God,' I heard him say. 'Quick, steer to starboard.' I did so, but turning into the wind seemed to make matters worse as the sail started to twist faster and faster around the stay until it was tightly entwined.

'Steer to port!' he yelled. I pulled on the tiller; suddenly we gybed, the boom crashing across and missing my head by a fraction of an inch and sending our dog tumbling to the floor of the cockpit. There then followed what seemed an eternity of gybing, going about, tugging at sheets and circulating arm movements as my husband gradually unfurled the sail.

As the sail broke free he yelled again, 'Sheet in.' Oh no! Not again, I thought.

By now my nerve had cracked and I could feel a lump rising in my throat. My eyes started to fill with tears and I knew I could take no more.

'Do you think we could take it down now, please?' I asked rather weakly.

'What the **** do you think I've been trying to do this past half-hour,' bellowed this red-faced, foaming-at-the-mouth MONSTER!

Anyone want to buy a cruising chute? • *Andrea Harmer*

Instant chaos

I was doing charter work on a 33ft yawl. We had just got under way; everything was set and drawing and I was going aft for a bucket to sluice the mud off the anchor which lay, with the chain, piled high on the foredeck. I was carrying the fender which had been used to buoy the anchor trip line and, on an impulse, I threw it over the side and shouted, 'Man overboard!'

Now, with hindsight, I realise that this was a mistake. At that time one of the popular theories for man-overboard drill was to gybe. The helmsman subscribed to this theory and reacted immediately. Unfortunately, he knew what to do but not how to do it. Without a thought of gathering in the mainsheet, he rammed the tiller across with all the force he could muster. It was a steel tiller and trapped and nearly broke the shinbone of his companion sitting opposite him the cockpit. The boom hurtled across and the ungathered mainsheet caught under the sliding hatch wrenching it off and, as the boat heeled, anchor and chain slid off the foredeck and plunged to the bottom.

Below, an unsuspecting member of the crew, together with five cups of coffee and the opened containers of sugar, milk and coffee, went flying as they obeyed the same laws of gravity as the anchor and chain. The anchor bit and we snubbed on the chain. The boat swung around and the boom hurtled back again, the mainsheet this time catching under the dinghy and slewing it athwartships as we brought up.

The only redeeming feature I could see in the whole incident was that it was only a fender that went over the side and not a person. • *Mike Peyton*

A very hot night

In mid-August last year I was on a singlehanded passage from Santa Cruz La Palma in the Canaries to Ponta Delgada in the Azores. *Bobtail*, my 25ft strip-planked sloop, was fitted with a Coventry Victor petrol engine but had no provision for battery charging, though I did have a small wind generator which could produce up to half an amp in winds in excess of 20 knots.

After two days becalmed, I was now running in about 15 knots true windspeed. Concerned about running my battery flat with the nagivation lights, I used the topping lift to haul my pressurised paraffin lamp up the backstay. Then, to stop the lamp swinging around too much, I attached about 10ft of elastic bungy to each side of it and hooked the bungy on to the wire guardrails either side of the cockpit.

It was 0500, the lamp was out and a rather sleepy, bemused skipper was trying to pre-heat and light it after refilling it. I'd clipped it back on to the topping lift and was hauling it up once more, stretching it nice and taut on its elastics, when, to my horror, it landed in my lap. To be more precise, the clip had come undone and the base had dropped and landed on my right kneecap, which I was

sure must be broken. The top of the lamp smashed on the cockpit sidebench and spewed paraffin under pressure into the cockpit.

It was very spectacular! I grabbed the base of the lamp and threw it over the side without thinking. Horror—the elastics were still attached and snagged on something. It flew about 4ft, came hurtling back at me still spewing burning paraffin over everything and lodged itself on the stern deck, wedged by the windvane. I was up to my knees in flames in the cockpit with a trail of burning paraffin on the sidedecks and sterndeck and more coming out.

I managed to get the thing over the side and pour water over everything in sight. Most of the paraffin had, in fact, burned away by then, and the cockpit paint and the mainsheet were just starting to ignite when I extinguished it.

I was lucky—slightly scorched hands and a bruised knee plus a heart rate of about 200. I did not sleep much more that night.

It is one of the drawbacks of singlehanded sailing that you have no one else to blame when things go wrong.• *Trevor Potts*

A lesson from authenticity

It takes seconds to do something stupid at sea, but often years to get into the frame of mind which makes such stupidity possible.

We never had guardrails or stanchions on *Shamrock*. Working

Essex smacks didn't have them, of course, and when she was yachtified in the Seventies we kept *Shamrock* looking as authentic as possible—with her foot-high bulwarks and exposed tiller—and trusted to luck. One day, a huge following sea swept the helmsman up the deck and, mercifully, wedged him under the staysail horse, but we continued to play at being latter-day intrepid smacksmen, although we were now sailing in blue water, far away from the Mersea mud.

We sold *Shamrock* and bought *Swift*, a delightful 30ft deep-keel gaffer, built by Philip & Son of Dartmouth in 1931, and fitted out below in teak and brass.

The previous owner, a parent, had corralled his children with stout stanchions and high guardrails. We took them off; they spoiled the line of the sheer. And anyway, spending your time at sea behind a wire fence seemed a funny way to sail.

It was a rainy March morning with a lot of wind when I took *Swift* from Dartmouth, where I'd bought her and set off for my mooring at Exmouth. A spring ebb was hammering out of the Dart and the wind was almost dead astern.

There were two of us, young Johnny at the helm, and myself up forward, tidying up after setting the mainsail and working jib... What followed sounds like a propaganda video for the prevention of nautical lunacy.

We scurried towards the narrow entrance guarded by the castles, where the wind always swirls unpredictably. In oilskins and wellies, I stood on the cabintop, my back to the mainsail, admiring the fast-receding view of Dartmouth through the rain.

Then, inevitably, the wind veered, and *Shamrock* gybed.

SWIFT

With a majestic haymaking stroke, the boom caught me at waist level and sent me soaring in a graceful arc in the general direction of Kingswear. River water is cold in March; boots fill quickly. A spring ebb and heavy oilskins give you a keen desire to be at home, by the fire, reading about other people's mistakes in *Yachting Monthly*. Johnny's dad, a sailing friend for years, had taught him well. He rounded up, dropped the main, fired up the engine, and came after me. Soon the bobstay was nudging comfortably at my side. I got a boot on it and was dragged aboard.

The guardrails are back in place and I'm busy trying to dismiss the incident as a momentary aberration after decades of accident-free and cautious yachting. Hopefully, though, a more important lesson has been learnt: when you're busy recreating a fantasy of yesterday's sailing, there's always the chance that you won't be around for tomorrow's. • *Tony James*

Following orders

I was planning to take my 40ft home-built ketch to the Isle of Wight for Cowes Week, to window shop and feast my eyes on the thousands of pounds translated into sleek hulls, gleaming fittings and luxury equipment.

Suspecting that berths were going to be at a premium, I agreed to take three out-and-out landlubbers along for the short trip from Lymington to the Island to assist in case of difficulties. Not knowing whether we would tie up alongside another yacht or the dock, pick up a mooring or drop the anchor, we rehearsed the three procedures separately and painstakingly until my crew knew exactly what to do in each case and would need only a quick command should I have to make a sudden decision on entering the crowded harbour.

We had a pleasant sail and nothing was left to chance as we neared our destination. Fenders were tied on to the rails, a bow- and stern-rope attached to the cleats were passed under the guardrails and coiled neatly, the anchor was laid on deck and a suitable length of chain flaked out. A boathook for picking up a mooring buoy lay ready on the cabintop. Slowly we motored into the port and I felt a twinge of pride as my crew stood smartly at their appointed stations.

I had nothing to fear; all my doubts had been needless; no one would ever suspect that they were total greenhorns.

I surveyed the various possibilities and decided that anchoring would be the best procedure.

'Get ready to drop the anchor!' I called out in the direction of the bow.

'Ahoy, *Mahon Mara*,' shouted a voice to port as an old friend of mine on a classic 60ft motor-sailer hailed me, waving an arm to indicate a berth alongside him. I put the tiller hard over and swung in under his starboard rail.

'Make fast,' I called. At which command a 45 lb rusty CQR anchor, followed closely by five fathoms of equally rusty chain, crashed its flukes on to the silvered teak deck of my friend's yacht.

I was dumbstruck. But we had planned to anchor, hadn't we?

• *Anna Woolf*

Brake failure

It had all started the previous day; the snag was, I didn't realise it.

We were chugging up Conyer Creek when there was a solid clunk as the propeller (variable pitch) hit something solid, and the engine stopped. Danny, always the optimist, turned the key and, to our surprise, the engine started and we were back in business. On we chugged.

The next day we had a boisterous sail to Whitstable where I had arranged to pick up my wife and then sail back to the Blackwater. Whitstable is a fishing harbour seldom used by yachts, so, as we motored in, the fishermen—and there seemed to be a lot of them—looked up with interest; the tourists—there were even more of them—also stopped to look. In fact we were the centre of attention. The harbourmaster appeared and beckoned; we headed towards him. Timed to a nicety, I gave the engine a touch of reverse…there was no reverse…whatever we had clunked the day before had seen to that.

We hit the harbour wall as only a 38ft ferro cement boat with plenty of way on can. The pulpit rose in greeting like a praying mantis to the harbourmaster…what more is there to say?

• *Mike Peyton*

Heads you loos

Imagine, if you will, the start of a fortnight's Brittany cruise aboard my Ohlson 38, with a mixed crew of six, three of whom were complete novices. We had just finished our first passage from Portsmouth to St Peter Port in typical July weather, south-west Force 5 with squally showers. The conditions had blunted the crew's enthusiasm slightly and I sensed that morale needed a boost before we continued on our next windward leg. A good run ashore ended with a slap-up meal rounded off with several nightcaps back on board. Eventually, a much happier crew retired to their bunks.

Now, everyone knows that boats can breed constipation, but just after lights-out the skipper realised that, for him at least, this problem was about to resolve itself and he slipped quietly into the heads. Ten minutes later, while pumping the handle, it became horribly apparent that a gallon of sea water had been pumped into the pan but nothing whatsoever had been pumped out. Further investigation suggested that the outlet pipe was hopelessly blocked and something must be done before the girls got up in the morning.

Still buoyed up by the nightcaps, I devised the cunning plan of disconnecting the pipework at the seacocks, unbolting the loo from its pedestal and then tipping the entire contents over the rail.

An hour later, all was going according to plan and I lifted the brimming loo, pipes carefully wedged vertically with my elbows. Problem—I'd forgotten to open the door of the heads. I was edging sideways towards the latch (still clutching the loo to my bosom), with my little finger extended when the cataclysm struck.

The pump handle of the loo caught the retaining catch of the large, rather ancient fire extinguisher in its bracket on the bulkhead. The extinguisher (dry powder) fell to the floor,

9

landed on its striker button and went off. There was a great
roaring noise, the extinguisher thrashed around my feet and the
very small heads compartment experienced a White Out.

Swearing wildly, I struggled to lower the loo into the rising
lake of dry powder and, just as I grabbed the extinguisher, it
finally exhausted itself.

There was a moment's deafening silence and then a sleepy
voice from the saloon called, 'Richard, everything OK in there?' I
fear my reply was even less printable than the rest of this
pathetic tale. • *Richard Close-Smith*

Trussed

Stepping the mast had been aborted owing to high winds and
now, having made a new appointment with the crane, I had to
motor the mile or so out in the dinghy to collect the boat and
bring her into the quay.

The omens were bad from the start. The train was half an hour
late, there were no taxis at the station and when I arrived at the
club I found I had left the dinghy shed keys behind. After finding
the club secretary, convincing him of my credentials and
borrowing his key, I at last had the inflatable afloat and the
outboard clamped in position. Time was desperately short—
would I make it? Would the crane driver wait? Was it going to
cost a fortune in overtime?

The outboard, a brand new Seagull, refused to start. The
alternative, a row against wind and tide, held little appeal or
hope. I tried every trick. I spoke kindly, I swore, I cajoled and
promised and still there was no spark of life. I cleaned the plug a
dozen times and checked the fuel supply to no avail. The beast
was not going to start.

In resignation I switched the fuel off, drained the carburretor
and decided to call it a day. With all my gear and the oars
transferred ashore I gave the engine one last pull before
unclamping; it roared into life. Rapidly I turned the fuel on,
grabbed my bag and oars and cast off, motoring across the
harbour at full throttle.

I suppose I had travelled about 200 yards when several things
happened simultaneously. The bows dipped, the dinghy appeared

to leap into the air and the outboard cut. It wasn't until I tried to tilt the engine that the truth dawned. The painter had fouled the propeller and now the dinghy drifted, its back arched like an angry cat.

Rowing was out of the question; sitting on top of the hump was too precarious. I could reach neither the propeller nor the painter at the bow. I was completely and utterly helpless, until inspiration dawned.

For once I had my knife in my pocket. I taped it onto the end of an oar and, after 10 minutes of sawing at the painter, with a twang and a splat as the dinghy landed, it came free.

And the crane? I arrived just as he was leaving and persuaded him to stay. As for the outboard, which I had bought cheap in a clearance sale, it was given the full pre-service checkover that I had neglected in the rush of fitting out. • *Andrew Bray*

The human painter

Ten years ago Andrew Bray, the then deputy editor of *Yachting Monthly* and I were cruising the West Country on the first *YM* cruise. We'd equipped the borrowed boat with Andrew's own Avon which had a peculiarly short painter and a brand new Seagull (see his Confession, page 10). He was touchingly protective about both.

The incident happened one evening in Dartmouth when we'd nipped ashore for some fish and chips and to phone our wives. The tide was high but ebbing so, just to be sure, we tied the short painter on to the end of a piece of chain dangling in the water from the edge of the quayside. With wives phoned and fish and chips eaten we were walking back to the quay when we met an old chum who twisted our arms to join him for a drink. One drink led to another and when we emerged,

four hours later, we both possessed that fortifyingly inebriated attitude of being ready to take on the world—nothing could be a problem any more.

The tide waits for no man, precious few women, and certainly no Avon dinghies. The cherished Avon and Seagull were now at the bottom of a deep wall (that hadn't, we noted, been there when we left), perched at about 45 degrees in a few inches of water.

The painter was tied to the chain about six feet below the quay and pulling up on the chain, even slightly, produced a meniscus around the now-fretting Bray's Seagull air intake. Some urgency was required as the tide was quickly receding and would soon dip the stern and drown the outboard in the process.

We weighed up the pros and cons painstakingly and verbally as only two drunks can, and put our plan into action.

Andrew, as the longer and lighter of the two, would manoeuvre himself over the edge of the quayside until I was holding him upside down by his ankles. He would then untie the painter and I would 'walk' him (gently, he suggested) towards the steps, fifty yards away, where our troubles would come to an end.

I suppose we were about half way to the steps, with Andrew complaining about a scratched nose, when he saw the humour of the situation and got the giggles. He was soon in convulsions, no doubt encouraged by the blood running to his head.

Looking back on it, it was inevitable that I'd start too. It all seemed so absurd, and the prospect of the local headlines if we made a mistake hilarious. 'We'll (giggle) write this up (giggle) one day', Andrew screeched to nobody in particular.

The almost schizophrenic change came suddenly. Andrew must have sensed that the grip on his ankles wasn't what it had been and reality (in the shape of an 18ft freefall skydive into the Avon or, if missed, six inches of water) made him stop laughing as abruptly as flicking a switch.

What followed was almost as funny: with graveness and reason (and impending injury) the Deputy Editor of *Yachting Monthly*, hanging upside-down from a West Country quayside, late at night, pleaded with me to regain my composure (and grip) by explaining the gravity of the situation. Gravity was not the word he should have used and it very nearly caused his downfall with a new wave of convulsive giggles. Fortunately he had yet to try out his flightpath when that twitchy nervous scream used by people facing death, or at least, serious injury calmed me down.

We made it to the steps and from there out to the boat but her high topsides were too much...one of us ended up spending some of the night in the Avon but neither of us can remember which. • *Geoff Pack*

Putting the boot in

We'd had a jolly evening ashore but the yacht lay at anchor half a mile away, her riding light a faint and distant pin-prick. It was easy rowing with a smart following breeze and the three of us sang loudly and joyously, then Jack stopped abruptly. 'My feet are wet', he announced. David concentrated owlishly. 'So're mine' he proclaimed. I was rowing, legs stretched straight out before me, I had boots on and felt justifiably smug; but not for long... Jack made another discovery, 'The floorboards are bloody floating', he howled. We were back in the days when boats had bungs—or in our case old corks—and ours was missing. We had no bailer, of course, other than their caps and my boots.

By this time we were beyond the shelter of the land and a sizeable sea was running, the yacht a hundred yards ahead and open sea beyond sea. I swung the dinghy and began to pull frantically back up-wind. It was hopeless, gradually we drew abeam and I tried to work over to her, only to lose ground in the process; and all the while the other two were bailing frenziedly. We almost didn't make it. Sobbing for breath, oars flailing I got her within an arm's reach of the stern.

What really riled me, however, was the discovery that they were still wearing dry caps, while my boots were wet through.
• *Des Sleightholme*

Boarding party

It would be wrong to say the weather was stormy, nor was the anchorage particularly exposed. But the Atlantic swell curled around the headland and drove straight up our Scilly Isles haven creating breakers on the beach and causing the yacht to pitch heavily with a corkscrewing motion as she lay half-bows on to the waves.

It would also be wrong to say the returning crew was inebriated but it had been a good run ashore and there was a jollity among the three on board which made small errors of judgement funny rather than annoying.

The yacht was of the modern type with high topsides but an aft bathing platform over which a boarding ladder had been lowered. When the boat was at rest the bottom two rungs would be below the water, the platform a couple of inches above and then there was a single rung on the transom to give a step up to the deck.

In the prevailing conditions, boarding over the side was next to impossible. The climb up the transom looked daunting enough as the stern lifted a couple of feet clear of the water with each wave before burying itself into the next with a crash.

It was not that the crew were unaware of the trickiness of the situation which confronted them: they were all experienced and had faced this situation before.

Perfect gentlemen both, the two men moved aside to let the lady crew member board first. She carefully sized up the situation, timing her move for the moment when the wave lifted the stern of the yacht and dropped the dinghy so that she could step neatly onto the platform and, with two more steps, would be up the transom and into the cockpit clear of the next surge of water.

After a couple of practice waves the moment arrived. The stern lifted, the dinghy dropped. She was a split second too slow. Her foot missed the bathing platform but caught on the first rung of the ladder. The stern continued to rise. She was plucked neatly out of the dinghy but lost her balance and slipped, only just gaining a toehold on the bottom rung. The yacht hovered for a brief, tantalising moment on the crest of the wave then swooped down, squirting the dinghy beyond reach of her searching foot.

The yacht plunged on down dunking her ankle, knee, waist and chest in inexorable, chilling sequence.

Then, as the stern rose once more, she let out a small shriek and swept over the transom with all the surefootedness of a mountain goat.

She was followed, a moment later, by two rather sheepish but dry men. • *James Jermain*

Of gaffs and goofs

We had not been married long and although we had done quite a bit of cruising in our Rival 34 it was not until we moved to the West Country that my wife and I acquired *Skylark*.

Twelve foot of humble Tupperware *Skylark* had come as part of our house purchase and we had spent the winter happily resuscitating her.

My wife had been new to sailing when she met me and, apart from a couple of afternoons on a Westerly Centaur, her only experience had been on the Rival. Dinghy sailing was a whole new world and she was keen to try it. I, on the other hand, had been sailing since I was a youngster in New Zealand. There was nothing to it, I assured her.

The first fine day in early spring found us down on the shore of the creek where the dinghy was moored to our outhaul. My wife's 13-year-old son was visiting and was just as keen as his mother to try the dinghy. With a gentle breeze and a flooding tide I felt conditions were ideal for a demonstration of sailing technique. So, while my crew stood attentively at the water's edge, I pushed off out into the stream to show my skill.

Skylark is gunter rigged and the little headsail was already hoisted, but with sheets loose, as the current caught the bow and drew me out into the river.

So far so good. I grasped the main halyard and heaved away to get the sail hoisted quickly. I was surprised at how heavy it seemed, and made a mental note to check the sheave later. My crew were waving from the shore but I was too busy to wave back.

By now I was in the mid-stream and moving faster up-river. I sheeted in the headsail quickly, and returned to haul on the main halyard but it was heavy as lead.

What were those two on the shore up to? Jumping up and down, pointing at the sky and shouting as if they were savages doing a rain dance. Really! Couldn't they see I was far too busy to watch their silly antics?

The wind had caught the half-hoisted main and the dinghy was now going at a good clip up the creek. Still I hauled at the halyard as hard as I could but it wouldn't go any higher. I cleated it off and decided to make for one of the many buoys in the river where I would sort it out.

I glanced toward the beach. What on earth was happening? They had gone mad! My wife was swirling her arms around and jabbing at the ground behind her and then up in the air. Stupid woman, how could I possibly see what was behind her from this distance? The boy was hugging his stomach and bending over, apparently in pain. Now they were clinging to each other as if he might collapse. I'd better get back at once.

I turned around to grasp the tiller but both rudder and tiller were gone. I couldn't believe my eyes, they had been there a minute ago, dammit. I was sure I'd put them on the transom; I remember pinching my finger as I dropped the rudder on to the pintles. Now there was nothing. Had the blessed thing broken loose? I stood up and cast around hoping to catch it floating nearby, but it was nowhere to be seen. Things were getting serious; the lad was sobbing on his mother's shoulder and she was trying to comfort him. Then he collapsed into one of the beached dinghies, still holding his guts. Good grief, appendicitis!

There was nothing for it but to get the oars and row back quickly. Forget the rudder, forget the manly display of seamanship, just get the main down and row. At that moment a windshift caused a sudden gybe and I ducked just in time as the boom swung across. Standing up again to go forward to lower the main, I came nose to nose with solid wood.

Looking skywards I was amazed to see the recalcitrant rudder hanging from the yard—a loop of halyard had snagged the tiller and, when I hauled away, had lifted the rudder clean off its pintles and taken it aloft. There it hung mocking me from on high.

It was only then that I caught the distant sound of laughter.

• *John Gibb*

The generation gap

Some people measure the difference between teens and adults in years elapsed; others measure it by the breakdown in communication. The age gap between my sister and myself was six years. I was the teenager, a sort of expendable foredeckhand; she was the owner, married to the skipper and had a babe at heel.

It was the time of the autumn equinox and we were bound down-Channel for some exotic clime. The run of storms was having a short intermission. Night had fallen and it was my watch. The steady beat of the Anvil light was falling astern. Fine on the bow the Portland light was sweeping the dark seas and, now and then, the Shambles light showed up between flurries of rain. Beyond the pale reflection of the compass binnacle, the cabin doors were outlined by the glow of the oil lamps swinging gently inside.

The doors were shut. It was quite pleasant, if a trifle lonely, to sit in the dark, feeling every fine shadow of balance pulse along the tiller to your fingers. It was almost as if the boat's lean wooden heart was talking to you.

Unexpectedly the hatch flew open, illuminating the mainsail. From below, my sister called out, but the wind took her words away to leeward and I could make no sense of them. Mystified, and drawn to the open hatch, I left the tiller, went forward and craned over the opening. Down below all looked normal. The skipper was asleep in the saloon. My sister was bent over the naked babe in the port quarterberth performing some maternal cleansing operation. Suddenly, she stood up and, with a casual gesture, flung something over her shoulder, up and out of the hatch.

As it spun through the air I recognised it as a fully laden disposable nappy just before it wrapped itself around my face with the deliberation of an octopus. In one horror-struck moment, I realised that the contents had a runny viscosity and that they formed an adhesive seal over my mouth and nostrils.

Mortified by this unkind assault, I staggered back, clutching at the nappy, bumping into the tiller before leaning right over the side. I must have resembled a victim of a 1917 gas attack, with boggling eyes, purple face and clutching hands. Before my oxygen completely ran out, I managed to unpeel the wretched thing and hang my head into the tops of the passing waves. The salt water laid bare my mouth, and I lay there, half in and half out of the boat gasping lung-fulls of air. The boat came about of her own accord and, with a clatter or two, settled herself hove-to on the other tack.

The change of course did not pass unnoticed by those below. My sister's head arose from the hatch and she surveyed the scene intently. Now able to breathe, I rose groggily from the rail, traces of the babe's alimentary wastes still clinging to my face. She looked me over and ran her eye up the mast, sarcasm growing in her eye.

'Am I supposed to tell the skipper that my kid brother is so seasick that he can't even take his turn on the helm?' Her voice was clearly pitched to instill some sense of decency in a worthless miscreant. 'Pull yourself together!' and the hatch slammed shut...

The unfairness of the rebuke left me so speechless that, for some time, I stood there with my mouth open, before resuming my duties and setting course to pass outside Portland. Somehow the night had lost its magic. • *A K Brassington*

Mid-day cowbuoy

Gibraltar to UK, ASAP. That was the brief. Our Rival 34 had languished under the shadow of the rock for three years. Now we must bring her home.

Thus, very early one morning in mid-July, we eased our way out of Sheppard's Marina for the last time. We slipped past the Naval Dockyard and silent destroyer pens, the unseasonal Levante sweeping us through the Straits and into the Atlantic.

About the fourth day out, we were motoring through a calm, the horizon hazy at two miles. Alone, on watch, I was trying to get the boat to steer herself with a contrivance of lines and bungy cord when something caught my eye.

'Something on the starboard bow,' I called.
'What sort of something?' came the patient
reply. 'A ship? Land? A whale?'
'Well, I don't know. It's disappeared now
but it looked like a large black-and-white buoy.'
'Don't be daft!' John's head came up through
the hatch, 'We're 100 miles offshore.'

Sally, never one to miss out, now appeared, sniffing the air like
a retriever.

'I can see it, too!' Her excited cry had us all scanning in the
direction of her pointing finger. 'Oh, it's gone again in the mist.'

'We'd better investigate,' said the skipper. 'It may be hazardous
flotsam that we should report, or even a liferaft with survivors.'

I went below to prepare nourishing broth and was absorbed
with my pans when the call 'All hands on deck!' had me up the
companionway like a rigger.

'There's your black-and-white buoy!'

Did I detect a note of scorn? Turning, I gasped in disbelief:
there, floating serenely by, like the fat lady in a naughty postcard,
was the deadest Frisian cow you ever saw. • *Jane Gibb*

A public dilemma

I was sitting in the heads one afternoon, quietly going over in my
mind all the stores and equipment that had been put aboard the
ship, and all the work that had been done on her, when, suddenly,
my blissful cogitation was rudely cut short.

A sharp gust of the gathering Force 7, a roll and a lurch of the
ship and, with a bang, the engine hatch cover, which had been
leaning against the oven, had altered course 90 degrees and was
firmly wedged against the lower half of the heads door. I was
trapped.

It was 30 April and for the May Day holiday I had planned to
sail *Jeopardy* down the Medway and up the Thames to Green-
wich. The previous night I had moved her from the half-tide
moorings in the marina almost to the end of a long, visitors' jetty.

In vain I tried to force the door. No family or friends were
expected and I had only been at the marina a short time—it
could be a very long time before anyone came to look for me.

The only porthole looked out on to the river which was deserted. There was no point in shouting, for who would be likely to come this far down the jetty in this weather? Besides, even standing right alongside, would they hear me?

The situation looked ominous indeed, but wait...all was not lost: the VHF was on the bulkhead just outside the door and tuned in to Channel 16. Could I reach the mike? With as much force as I could muster it was just possible to force the top half of the door an inch or two from the frame and, with two fingers, reach the mike cord and ease it up to the top of the door.

Finally I had it in with me. But who to call and how to describe the situation? I knew only two people with boats on the river who kept a radio watch while onboard, so out went the first call. Three times over a period of 5-10 minutes I called but with no joy. I switched to the next craft, still with no response.

Then I tried, 'Will any craft in the Rochester area come in please.' This was repeated with a deafening lack of response. Although people in the clubhouse and on boats only a few feet away heard my calls, no one replied.

Finally, it was time to take the bull by the horns. It would have to be a Pan Pan call so out went the ship's name once more. This time the reply was immediate.

'North Foreland to *Jeopardy*, can you change channel?'

'Sorry no can do, I am trapped aboard my ship and could only just manage to reach the mike. There is no way that I can reach the switch to alter the channel.'

'Describe the nature of your emergency, where you are, and what we can do for you.'

'I am tied up at the visitors' berth of such and such marina. I had the engine hatch cover off when I went to the loo; the ship rolled and the cover has jammed the door. No one knows that I am here (though by this time scores must have done). Could you please 'phone the marina and have someone come down and release me.'

Then, to top everything, without so much as a tremor or even hint of a chuckle in his voice, this gentleman from the Coastguard, replied, 'I think we can manage to do that sir, but would you mind giving me the name of your ship again?'

I could only reply, 'I am in *Jeopardy*.'

'Very good sir, someone will come for you within 20 minutes.'

Twelve months later, people still point and say, 'There's the man who got locked in the loo.' Asked what they know of it they often reply that they heard it all on their radio but thought the call was a hoax.

I have since sold the ship and changed my name. • *J P Loft*

'Foreign' affairs

It was our first time of going 'foreign' foreign. Well, the Isle of Wight seemed foreign after a nine-hour beat into an occasional Force 1.

In fact, it was our first time out of Chichester Harbour. We had several weekends of teach-yourself sailing behind us and it was the start of our Easter holiday. Having read everything from 'How to build and sail your own boat' to 'Heavy weather sailing', we were keen to put theory into practice.

Somehow the real thing was different. We realised that eleven tacks to clear the end of Ryde Pier wouldn't earn us a place in the Admiral's Cup team, but we had finally made it into Wootton Creek. The last mile or so in the dark had been a new and stressful experience, as had our first attempt to anchor.

A three-course meal from a single-burner stove was no mean feat and the first tot of rum in a plastic cup released the tension of the day. I checked the anchor and inflated the dinghy. My wife was asleep by the time I had stripped and crawled into my bag.

I awoke in a panic—the noises, lights and vibration seemed on top of us. 'Get on deck—get the anchor up!' I screamed as I struggled to the outboard. The ferry was headed straight for us.

For the first time I realised how good my wife was in an emergency. The choice of the only article of clothing she had thrown on was unfortunate, but we didn't notice at the time. She was making excellent progress with the anchor chain when somebody hit the lights. To our night-adjusted sight, it was as bright as day.

Two impressions struck me: the beauty of the vision on the foredeck as she strained at the anchor wearing only my string vest; and the absence of any real danger—the ferry had berthed at a pier several yards behind us.

It was the first time I had seen her angry—really angry.

• *K D Sowden*

How not to drop your anchor

Marina di Carrara on the north-west coast of Italy is a busy commercial port famous for its nearby marble quarries. It has a large area reserved for yachts and was our destination for the night.

Mooring Mediterranean-style usually means securing bow or stern to a quay or pontoon with an anchor at the other end. Rarely do you have the opportunity to go alongside but you have to be prepared for all eventualities.

George, our occasional but reliable part-time crew, had done his usual meticulous preparations and we were ready for anything. We had experienced problems with the anchor chain running out, so we had it flaked out on deck and the Bruce lay on the bow roller ready to go. All it needed was a push.

Entering Carrara, we were met by two young men in the yacht-club dinghy who indicated we were to go between two moored yachts, bow to a pier, and pick up a buoyed line for our stern. This involved a 90-degree turn in a congested area which was executed in a careful manner.

Then the club boat decided to be helpful. It picked up the buoyed line and took a tight turn with it on our starboard cockpit cleat, pulling our stern to starboard and our bow to port.

What happened next I would prefer to forget. Our bow roller passed between the cockpit guardrail wires of the Italian yacht to port and, with a loud 'twang', snagged itself on the lower wire. Our boat stopped dead. The Bruce, however, had other ideas and kept going. One fluke hit a chromed sheet winch a glancing blow, producing a melodious bell-like chime, and then toppled on to a wooden cockpit seat. There, it skittered along before

dropping with a crash on to the cockpit grating.

The commotion had an immediate effect: two men bounded into the cockpit from below, a look of absolute disbelief on their faces as they viewed our bow hanging over them and an anchor at their feet. They stood transfixed as over 100 feet of 5/16in short-link calibrated anchor chain went 'chug-chug, rattle-rattle, chuff-chuff' and deposited itself over and around their bare feet. A grey cloud of dust and dried mud settled on them slowly.

It was our soon-to-be neighbours who were the first to recover. After extricating their feet, they lifted one guardwire and pushed our bow back. They then grabbed armsful of chain and dumped it overboard followed, finally, by the offending anchor.

By the time we were properly secured in our berth, the Italians seemed quite amused by the whole incident and, no doubt, had a rather good tale to tell in the yacht club. Needless to say we stayed away.

By good fortune there was no damage done and we were left with no worse than injured pride.

And the moral of the story? Beware unsecured anchors and do not try to anchor in someone else's cockpit. • *Peter Jennings*

Beware the sunny day

It was many years ago...very soon after the end of the 1939 war. The days were golden, I had a lot of accumulated leave. I also had the ketch *Manora* and she was my pride and joy.

She had lovely teak hatches with bars which allowed the incautious to sit on them and not break the glass; she had a tiller with a Turk's head carved on to its end, an engine that worked occasionally and a beautiful 9ft clinker dinghy. I loved each and every feature and she was mine; my very first boat with a cabin— a boat that would sail the seas. Which, in due course, she did...though it was touch and go.

I had taken friends from our home mooring off Rhu pier, down through the East Kyle, to Tighnabruaich. We had brought a sumptuous hamper with wine and lobster and early strawberries for lunch, and cucumber sandwiches and Dundee cake for tea, and we had enjoyed every moment of the cruise.

My guests, however, were workers and had to take their noses back to their grindstones on Monday morning. I saw them off on the Sunday afternoon steamer to Gourock and looked forward to making my way home by myself. I like singlehanded sailing.

Monday morning was as fine as Sunday had been, and I meandered back past the Burnt Isles and Rothesay and Toward Point. I clearly recall how pleased I was when I went about and found that I could just lay the Cloch lighthouse. The Clyde was blue and sparkling; steamers with brightly coloured funnels and wisps of brown smoke bustled about and all was peace. The wind dropped more and more until we were only just moving through the water. The tranquillity was delicious. *Manora* steered herself— she almost always did, except sometimes on a run. I dozed.

Half an hour later nothing had changed and I decided to take a book into the dinghy and doze there: it would make a change of scene, and I could admire my darling ketch, all sails set. I dozed again; the almost windless afternoon was warm and wonderful.

It was the sudden increase of speed that woke me. Instead of gliding through the water we were whooshing through it. The wind had come back up—Force 3 perhaps, and had veered a point. We were no longer weathering the Cloch Point; we were aiming at the rocky ledges and boulders to the south of it. No matter, I thought, I'll just have to make another tack, and I made

my leisurely way forward to grasp the painter, haul back alongside and clamber inboard.

The dinghy, however, would have none of it. As soon as I got forward of the rowing thwart she dug her nose down and started to take water over the bow. I knew perfectly well that the painter was a disgrace...any semblance of swamping the boat at this speed and the rope would part in an instant.

I looked at the rocks approaching, I looked at *Manora* roaring along with a bone in her teeth, and steering herself, as ever, perfectly. I stretched and str...r...e..etched like a telescope, to try to reach the painter from abaft the thwart but my arm was at least a foot too short. I prayed for a lull in the breeze and it didn't come. I tried crawling along the bottom boards under the thwart instead of over it and, just when I was nearly within grasping distance, over the stemhead washed a wave. I beat a slow and undignified retreat, considering whether to attempt going overside and haul my way forward on the gunwale, but that seemed silly too. The rocky ledges were now very close indeed and we were making 6 knots.

The lull in the breeze (when it finally came) was momentary, but quite long enough. I was back and inboard as quickly as any kangaroo could have done it...but I've never been to sleep in a towing dinghy since. • *Peter Hamilton*

The creep

It was 6.30 in the morning. I crawled out of my bunk and got dressed as my wife of only a few weeks slept on.

The morning was perfect. Not a cloud in sight and just a gentle breeze as I started the engine, which fired immediately. A good day in prospect!

I left the engine turning over, unfastened the for'ard mooring rope and climbed aboard the boat alongside us to tie it off. I did the same with the stern rope, making sure the ropes were fast in every way.

I turned around to climb on to our yacht but...she wasn't there!

It was then that I remembered the creep in the gearbox. Earlier in the season, I had found that when the gearbox was cold and the oil thick, the gears would to creep a little; when the oil was warmer, then everything was OK. I had forgotten and the yacht was motoring away at yards a second. PANIC!

I whispered my wife's name—no response. I called my wife—no response. I shouted to my wife—she responsed. She leapt up from below, saw the problem immediately and moved the gearbox lever astern...everything under perfect control, bless her.

'Thank God,' I thought as I watched the boat being expertly manoeuvred by this ravishing maiden, wearing only the flimsiest of see-through nighties, 'Thank God it's only 6.30 in the morning; this could have been very embarrassing.'

As the yacht came alongside, I hastily re-fastened the mooring ropes and climbed into the cockpit to pull myself together. 'Boy,

am I glad that little cock-up is over,' I thought, when, as if by instinct, I looked up at the harbour wall.

There they stood: the local fishermen, all in a row, arms crossed and with big grins all over their faces.'Do you do this every day?' shouted one of them. I slid on to the cockpit well, and eased my way into the cabin for words of comfort from my wife...the look on her face told me that, instead, a very large depression was heading my way. • *K J Rogers*

The elegant garbage collector

My wife and I and our two young children had spent a quiet evening aboard our small sloop, *Bydand*, in the anchorage at Edgartown, Massachusetts. One of the guidebooks states that in the anchorage one is 'surrounded by some of the most elegant yachts of the Atlantic coast'.They were, indeed, all around us, most of the crews taking advantage of the hospitality of the Edgartown Yacht Club that has an attractive 19th-century club house offering meals and launch service.The town itself offers a morning garbage collection.

I was sitting reading *Riddle of the Sands*, lost somewhere with Davies and Carruthers among the Frisian Islands, as the sun lifted up over Chappaquiddick Island to the east. On the seat next to me was a particularly odoursome bag of garbage, with the remains of some fish we had dined on the night before.

I glanced up every now and then, hoping to see the town garbage boat. Finally I saw a long vessel moving through the fleet with what appeared to be a solitary figure at the helm. The garbage scow at last! I waved to gain the skipper's attention and when he saw me he turned and approached slowly. I called to my wife, for 50 cents to pay him and picked up the awful smelling bag, just as the boat gently touched our port side. Quickly I lifted the bag over our lifeline and thrust the money into the man's outstretched hand. From what little I could see, the helmsman seemed quite well dressed...

I reached for my glasses, put them on and realised my mistake. Drifting slowly away was the elegant Edgartown Yacht Club launch, the captain in his blazer and yachting cap standing with the garbage bag still held in the hand of a very outstretched arm, his other hand clenching 50 cents, and an incredulous expression on his face.

We have never been back. • *Michael Wallace Gordon*

Outboard overboard

I keep my 39ft yacht *Brazil* on a mooring in a normally lonely bay on the north-west coast of Scotland where all supplies and maintenance materials have to be taken out by dinghy.

On arrival, the technique is to tie the dinghy alongside the yacht, unclip the outboard from the transom and lift it on to the stern deck, propeller end first. So far, so good, but on this particular day, as I lifted the engine, the dinghy slowly moved away from the yacht, leaving me holding the outboard over the side with nothing to support its bottom end.

I distinctly remember plunging head first into the sea and going down quite a depth, still clutching the outboard. There was no way I was going to leave £250's-worth of Yamaha on the muddy sea-bed, so I surfaced, still clutching it.

Grabbing the dinghy gunwale with my spare hand, I worked my way slowly around to the stern, but I could not lift the outboard into the dinghy with one hand, and, if I let go of the dinghy, I sank.

The only piece of rope which might have provided a hand-hold, or something to support the engine, was the bitter end of the dinghy painter, and that was just out of reach on *Brazil*'s deck. Eventually, I managed to get the outboard between my thighs and hang on to the transom with both hands. But I still had the problem of what to do next.

Luckily, a friend and his wife were pottering around in their inflatable a few hundred yards away and came to help.

It proved surprisingly difficult to get myself and the outboard back into the dinghy and nowadays I take more care when engaged in the outboard- parking manoeuvre. I realised later that the reason why the procedure used without difficulty on numerous occasions had failed this time was that there was absolutely no wind. Previously, there had always been enough breeze to keep the dinghy tight in alongside the yacht.

• *M K Tucker*

Who'd have thought it?

The wind was south-east Force 4 when we arrived on board at
10am. I prepared the craft for sea, and raised the mainsail. *Vida II*
picked up into the wind, and I dropped the mooring and dinghy
off to leeward.

I noticed Ted's dinghy on his mooring, but his boat was not in
sight. We both normally sail singlehanded and I reflected that it
was a poor state of affairs that Ted, who is in his seventies, was
still getting out to sea before me.

I sailed fast to the mouth of the river. Out at sea it was a bit
bumpy, but I was able to tie the tiller and sail towards the
shipping lane. Ahead was a craft hove-to, just outside the main
channel. I carried on sailing and noticed that there was no sign of
life on board. Half an hour later there was still no sign of life.

I was close enough to recognise Ted's boat. I headed towards
her, thinking that he might have gone over the side or had a heart
attack. I would have informed Thames Coastguard, but my radio
was out of order. I sailed around the boat, but still no one
appeared. Since it had been an hour ago that I had first sighted
her, I decided to pull away, furl the foresail, drop the main and go
alongside under power. It would not be easy in a choppy sea
with Ted's boat hove-to.

With extra fenders rigged, and bow and stern lines outside the rigging, I went alongside. At the critical moment a biggish sea hit us and I ran into the boat with a bump. I was about to jump, when Ted, red-faced and in a state of undress, came charging out of his cabin, shouting abuse at me and telling me to push off.

Embarrassed, I grabbed my tiller and pulled away. It was then that I observed a vivacious blonde female in his cabin.

• *David Edmonds*

Jellyfish do sting

We were about 200 miles north of Bermuda en route from the Virgin Islands to Falmouth when the trailing electronic log stopped reading yet again.

After finishing my 'Happy Hour' fizzy American beer I generously opted not to wake the skipper from his siesta. Instead, in the hot sunshine, I sat down to pull the cable and impeller aboard and spend a few minutes unwinding and scraping gelatinous, stringy blobs of Portuguese Man-of-War jelly fish from the unit's blades and shaft.

A job well done, I chucked the cable and impeller overboard and made sure that the log was providing a realistic reading. Perfect.

It was time to transfer the processed fizzy beer to the sea. I sauntered casually over to the rail, unzipped and relieved myself. Contented, I sat down to enjoy a good read. Minutes later I was jumping about the cockpit, hair standing on end, sweating at the incredible stinging sensation of my most private parts. I had 'stung myself' with the Man-of-War venom left on my fingers.

Many rinses later, and after liberal applications of Johnson's Baby Powder, I reflected that there should be a sign on the guardrails saying 'In the interests of safety, please wash your hands!'

• *Richard Manly*

Sailing looks so simple

Like many things, when performed by experts, sailing looks simple enough. It looks exciting and enjoyable too. Irresistible, in fact.

On holiday, my 14-year old son and I 'had a go' on the sailing pond at Southwold. This was safe enough for anybody. The boats were tubs with lugsails and the water was hardly deep enough to swim in, let alone drown. If you got becalmed, or on a lee shore, you could use a paddle to get out of trouble or embarrassment. But if there was anything more than the lightest breeze, the man in charge wouldn't let his boats out. 'Too gusty today!' he'd say.

It whetted our appetite for something more like the real thing. Thus, on a day trip, a few miles down the coast to Aldeburgh, we found a wide, open estuary where there was real sailing—and sailing boats for hire.

There was a stiff breeze and I was surprised when a young chap agreed to let us have a dinghy for an hour at quite cheap rates. 'Have you done any sailing?' he asked. 'We've done a bit on a lake,' I said, with an air which may have reassured him and surprised me. 'Lake' sounded better than 'pond'.

He stepped the mast, rigged the sail, and all was ready. I said I thought we'd better have lifejackets, just in case. He made no demur and routed out a couple of moth-eaten specimens from his cluttered shed. I helped pull the boat down to the water, and my son and I climbed in.

I used the oars to get us out of the shallows while my son fixed the rudder, lowered the centreboard, and pulled in the mainsail to catch the wind. It didn't need much catching. It was there all the time, catching us.

We sailed in fine style. I just sat in the middle of the boat and let my boy manage everything. We smacked over the waves with no trouble at all. It was exhilarating and as simple as I had thought it to be.

Then it was my turn to have a go. My son turned into the wind and we changed places gingerly. This was when the trouble started. I tried to turn the boat around and sail back. But the darn thing wouldn't go round; it only seemed to want to go further from the distant shore.

We humoured it for a while. Then I tried again. And, what with one thing and another, I got the mainsheet wrapped around me so that I couldn't move either myself or the sail. It threatened to be fatal. The wind caught us and water came aboard, uninvited.

I don't remember what I said, but my son acted promptly. He shifted his weight and we righted ourselves. I sat there like a trussed chicken and would have gone down with the boat, not so much in the tradition of the sea as in the ignominious incompetence of the ignorant amateur.

After agonising seconds I was freed. We managed to turn the boat and started back. Everything was plain sailing once more. Plain? The lee shore was getting nearer all the time. I couldn't understand it and, indeed, before I began to, there was an ominous grating and we were aground.

We had escaped real danger, but shame and ridicule lay ahead. Everything went wrong. Each time I tried to push off from the shore the wind pushed us back. I couldn't lower the sail because it was tied to the mast. My boy had the presence of mind to pull the centreboard up. The rudder nearly floated away before he could grab it, and I nearly lost a rowlock when it came away with an oar.

We were well and truly stuck. Any idea of sailing back in triumph was gone. Now it was a matter of getting back at all. Slowly and laboriously I rowed towards our departure point. It was tough going.

Suddenly a gun went off. Good lord, they weren't shooting at us, were they? No. It was the finish of a yacht race and we were in danger of being run down by the leading yachts. Was there no end to our misfortunes? We finished up at the yacht club slipway, and walked back to tell the man where his boat was. He charged us 50p extra for rowing it back and made nothing of it.

We slunk away, thinking it cheap at the price. • *Will Garnett*

Mudlarking

Pristine with her resprayed topsides and newly oiled woodwork, *Three Fishes* was at last ready to return to Ramsgate. She had spent the summer at Conyer Creek, a dribble of a river which seemed to be in a permanent state of low tide.

We left on a Spring high with clear skies and a north-east Force 3-4. I felt familiar with Conyer, which I had negotiated successfully several times. We cast off and motored out gently towards the withies that mark the channel. Then, as I surveyed the creek, I had a total mental blackout.

The only withy I could see was way off to starboard, almost alongside a rusting old barge. It felt horribly wrong, but I headed straight for it.

Three Fishes is a Watson motor-sailer and a heavy boat—even at 2 knots she managed to dig herself into the mudbank with the skill and speed of a badger. It was the highest tide for the next four months.

The locals, highly amused, put out a launch to attempt a tow. *Three Fishes* sat bolt upright on her long keel, refusing to budge in any direction. As we wearily abandoned ship and paddled to the shore, I noticed the first strands of marsh grass beginning to poke through the surface around her hull. Ten minutes later, *Three Fishes*, like a latter-day Ark, was sitting serenely in the middle of a sea of green fronds.

The next morning, a digging party from Bay Class Yachts and the biggest tug in the creek pulled her off. I went to the Ship Inn, not daring to watch. Anthony, an extra crew member was already there. Eager to maximise my discomfort he announced loudly as I entered the bar, 'I say, aren't you the skipper of that boat in the field over there?'

Amid much hilarity, one of the locals sidled over. 'I hope for your sake you get her off,' he said.

'Why's that?' I snarled.

'Well the last bloke what done that got sued by the farmer. Three of his sheep died after licking the anti-fouling off the bottom.'

The pub erupted and I left, never to return. • *Andy Ward*

Smuggling Clyde

Leaving a remote island in the Pacific marked the end of a glorious three-month cruise with Guam marked on the chart as our final destination. Our 70ft ketch cut a fine figure as she sliced effortlessly through the water carrying her skipper, four crew and Clyde.

Clyde, along with half a dozen other deliciously succulent coconut crabs, was presented to us by the local islanders on the morning of our departure. Needless to say such an offering was promptly devoured at lunch-time with freshly baked bread...all except Clyde. He was just too big.

No matter how we prodded and poked, we just couldn't get him into the pot, so he was spared. Seemingly resigned to his unexpected trip, Clyde made himself comfortable under the cockpit table, carefully fastened to a makeshift harness with plenty of scope for stretching his legs, should the need arise. This proved to be rather unnerving during the night watch as you were never quite sure where he was and the thought of one's toes being nibbled certainly kept you awake.

A week later, we were motoring into Guam Harbour. Having made radio contact, we could see Customs and Immigration officials closing fast on our port bow and made ready for them to board. All of a sudden, there was Clyde taking his usual afternoon stroll around the deck! How on earth were we going to explain an enormous tree crab sunning itself on our boat, let alone talk our way out of the huge fines and possible detention for smuggling live animals. We panicked! I unclipped Clyde and charged like a madman in and out of cabins looking for a suitable hiding spot. It was fruitless. I returned on deck, just in the nick of time, to slip him into the spare fishing box underneath the cockpit table.

We all held our breath and introductions were made.

The next two hours were spent shifting nervously from one foot to the other as the officials made their rounds and we docked alongside the main wharf. All was going well; the Customs official sat in the cockpit chatting happily to our skipper and a welcoming drop of brandy was poured. Hands were shaken and everyone stood up to go ...disaster!

The Customs official had inadvertently kicked the incriminating fishing box as he rose and a distinct scraping sound could be heard from within.

We all went very pale.

He stooped to investigate.

'What do we have here?'

We all took a good slug of brandy.

'Oh a coconut crab. You should try cooking it you know, they're quite delicious!' And with that he quietly departed with a knowing smile. • *Ruth Donaldson*

Wallet overboard

'Gas off, batteries off, seacocks closed, boat locked!' The end of a dismal summer's cruise. *Sandaig* was tide-ridden on her mooring at Tighnabruaich, in the West of Scotland, a cable offshore. The streaming rain put a gloss on the oilies which had been our daily rig for June, covering five layers of clothing.

Checks over, I turned aft, untied the dinghy from the port quarter and inverted it to tip five gallons of rainwater into the West Kyle.

'Is that your wallet in the sea?' asked the mate in a conversational tone (her eyesight not being matched by her sense of urgency).

Indeed it was. It had apparently fallen from my hip pocket into the dinghy when I had gone ashore the previous evening. Now, small and vulnerable, it was drifting rapidly downtide.

Under threat of pecuniary loss the mate's mind works rapidly. 'Quick, get the bucket!' she said.

With my left hand, I fished the bucket with its long lanyard out of the stern locker even as my right hand attempted a rapid hitch of the dinghy painter to the pushpit. The mate, meanwhile, mindful of emergency drills, was fully occupied keeping her eye on the WOB. All else was left to me. Despite a few failures, a final despairing cast with the bucket lanyard at full stretch secured a soggy but intact wallet.

'Thank heavens for that.' I turned my attention to the dinghy. No dinghy. My hitch had clearly been a slippery one.

Looking in the direction of the current, I saw the dinghy, already 100 yards away, heading for a closely moored group of boats down the anchorage and well inshore. Both anchorage and shoreline were devoid of human life. Visions of an enforced and possibly lengthy sojourn in a damp boat presented themselves to both of us. With a surprising and uncharacteristic degree of magnanimity, the mate eschewed strong language and merely said quietly, very quietly, 'What do we do now?'

I knew that, once inshore, and among a cat's-cradle of moorings, the dinghy would be inextricable and with wind and tide in its favour, speed was of the essence.

That power of decision natural to skippers reasserted itself. 'Open the boat, start the engine, cast off!' In less than a minute the Sabb thumped into life with its usual teeth-chattering vibration, we were off the mooring and in a graceful sweep *Sandaig* was propelled at top speed towards her silent companion. At the last possible second the mate made a masterful pick-up of the errant dinghy and, with the triumphant roar of full power, we surged back against the tide to our starting point.

Safe again and honour restored, I permitted myself some modest self-congratulation.

'That was a pretty slick manoeuvre.'

'Hmm,' said the mate, looking down below and sniffing, 'Did you open the engine water seacock?' • *D A Moore*

Bobcat express

I recall a thoroughly unedifying experience more than 20 years ago when I owned No1 Bobcat. Unlike most Bobcats, it was a rather hairy lightweight ply boat with a massive high-roached, fully-battened main and a genoa which I had unwisely but enthusiastically purchased.

In those days, all cats, and there were not a lot of them, were anathema to monohull sailors, but I was surprised to see the Solent so quickly deserted. Then it dawned on me that the wind was getting up...out came the portable radio and, sure enough, there was a bad weather forecast.

I decided not to return to Shoreham, but to leave the boat in Chichester and take the train home—a good, responsible decision with Chichester being close by.

The forecasters were right. It was piping up. At the time, hand-held wind gauges were fashionable, but ours had been under-reading since the children had been competing to see who could blow hardest and the saliva had made it sticky.

We were off Cowes and Chichester was 'only over there', downwind; we were going like a train, as the island's lee effect reduced. Clear of the island, the apparent wind still seemed quite acceptable, but the speed was not something my newly acquired Autohelm could cope with and the idea of reducing sail looked like a major challenge. 'We'll take it all down going up the Emsworth Channel', I thought.

Chichester Bar Buoy was approaching quite quickly and we were going to have to gybe. My son was keen and willing and, bingo, after a fight with the genoa, it was done, inducing a well-deserved sense of confidence.

Some stragglers were still entering the harbour, virtually standing still on the tide which was sluicing out as we raced in waving and smiling. I did not then understand that the tide reduced our speed over the ground, thereby increasing the apparent wind and inevitably the speed through the water. Like it or not, I was committed.

It had been quite choppy, so the swirling wave ahead did not particularly concern me. We lifted over the front but tilting down the other side was assisted considerably by the wind in the high-roached main. The bows dug deep into the next swirling mound

and the boat stopped. It felt as though we had hit a wall.

The next few seconds shook my new-found confidence with a crash as everything was flung forward. The mast had only one forestay and two backstays, causing an enormous twang, but only cracking it. The genoa sheets pulled the camcleats out of the ply, letting fly a thrashing genoa. My son crashed to the cockpit floor, having been offending no one but, rather, busying himself clearing up the main track lines from the gybe.

Forward buoyancy caused the bows to shoot upwards, shovelling up the top half of the disturbed water and sending it aft as a green wave. I ducked in behind the cabin and the wave landed in the cockpit on top of my prostrate son. He had always believed in the biblical assertion that 'the sins of the fathers are visited on their children'. He believes, conversely, that his rationale comes from having to deal with the problem of an irrational father. At this point his sweet reasonableness deserted him, together with his keen willingness, and I engaged myself in a new fight with the genoa. • *Ken Pack*

Highly strung

Time to leave Southwold. Our cruise from Shotley had been the first real trip for me, my wife and our two boys in *Felisonca*, our Jaguar 27. For three days we had pottered about, caught crabs, and made friends with the experienced Dutch crews around us.

I was determined to leave that tricky harbour, with its racing tides, in a seamanlike manner. All lines were shortened, springs cast off.

My wife inquired about the line going across the cockpit. 'Belongs to them,' I said, waving to the Dutch crew a few feet behind us.

It didn't. *Felisonca* moved forward, and stopped. That line was another spring, put on one night and overlooked. It was like a guitar string. The bow rope was off. If I was quick, I could get on the jetty, run forward, catch it and pull the boat back.

I was too slow, and I was now on the pier, the current was slewing *Felisonca* around, and a shattering collision between my topsides and the bow gear of the Dutch ketch was inevitable.

The Dutch were marvellous, slipped the spring and *Felisonca* drifted, undamaged but skipperless, out into the middle of the stream.

Luckily, I prefer to let others take the helm. My elder son had spent time on the tiller, up and down the Orwell and the upper reaches of the Deben, although never in a current like this. He kept calm, got the spring on board, gave it some welly, got steerage way, moved to the other bank, spun her around and headed downriver. Could he pick me up somewhere before Harwich?

The Dutchman invited him to come alongside, rather than aim for the jetty. I waited, hanging off the ketch's shrouds until, balancing the throttle against the current, No 1 son brought her in with a touch that would not have broken an egg. I stepped aboard.

You could have cut the silence in the cockpit with a knife...and that's what I always now have handy—a great big kitchen knife. I won't need it; you don't forget that sort of laxity.

• *Ray Heath*

Fickle finger

It was early afternoon and already St Peter Port Marina had no pontoon space for catamarans. We moored against the wall, by the main road, and prepared to dry out. The skipper was below writing the log when, suddenly, an electronic alarm sounded.

Beep! Beep! Beep!

'Low voltage,' he thought. 'Better run the engine.' He called to the crew in the cockpit. 'Is there still some water?'

The crew, seeing water over the marina sill, reported that there was and the skipper started the engine, wondering vaguely why the voltage should be low when the last hour of the passage had been under power. The voltmeter read Normal, the beeping stopped, and the crew retired to his cabin for a sleep. Lulled by the idling engine, the skipper dropped off too. All was peace. But not for long.

Silently the accommodation filled with smoke. The skipper awoke with a start and shouted 'Fire!' He stopped the engine and opened up the engine hatch as the crew leapt into action, grabbing a fire extinguisher. The tide was out, the boat had dried out, and with no cooling water the flexible exhaust pipe was smouldering. Ruefully, he set about fitting a new length of

armoured hose, but cut his hand badly and ended up in the local casualty department. What else could go wrong?

Six hours later, wound stitched, blood washed off the deck, and the boat floating at road level, he was enjoying a well-earned Scotch in the cockpit, when the evening quiet was rent once again by the dreaded alarm. Looking up, his eyes lighted on a man, only yards away, with his finger on the button of the pedestrian crossing. 'Beep! Beep! Beep!' The lights went red and the traffic came to a halt. • *P F Middleton*

Lighting-up time

Early on, we very nearly hit the Channel One buoy in the dark and in response its light flashed on. Just a slight delay with lighting up time.

Not so the next problem, which came trundling and clanking out of the mist and murk close by. No chance of missing this one—a veritable Piccadilly Circus of lights, twinkling and flashing in all directions. What should we do? What was it? Nothing in book or memory matched this lot: reds, whites, greens in profusion, like a voyaging disco-and-bingo hall for off-duty pilots.

There was just something about the shape, a hulking, heavy-shouldered ship, menacing.

'I think,' I said hesitantly, 'we'll go well around this. It may be towing something.'

We did and it was. About half a mile astern of it came a huge, nearly submerged, entirely blacked-out 'thing'. Round, smooth, featureless. An oil tank? A submarine? Thoughts of the length of steel cable twanging out in the dark gave us the shivers.

Never again, I said. However weird or complex the lights, I'm going to be able to say, right off, first glance, 'It's a raft-up, having a party', or 'It's an unlit fisherman smoking a pipe.' That sort of thing.

In pursuance of this high ideal, I was determined to look out for anything really interesting or unusual on one of our many ferry trips to France, a safe enough place from which to make mistakes.

Sitting in the car, on the quayside, I watched a huge P & O ferry inch its way into a berth against a gale which had every

shroud and halyard in Portsmouth shrieking and banging. Slowly the ferry strained against its springs and came to a halt, at which instant up flashed a truly novel set of masthead lights. Whites over reds, reds over greens, two orange (orange?) laterals, all kinds of things.

No hurry, I thought. No diving below for the book, no panic. Keep calm. What was it? Frying tonight? Surely not on a P & O ferry. Towing? Cable laying? Not under command? Aground? Foul this side?

Tensely, I explained the seriousness of the situation to my almost non-sailing wife: how all Yachtmasters should know everything there was to know about lights and signals. My heart was accelerating dangerously. She didn't seem in the least frightened.

'That?' she said, glancing upward casually, 'it's a Christmas tree!'
• *M J Lee*

Loco line

A friend, now a retired master mariner, was but a boy when he embarked on his first voyage on a schooner. It was in the days when coal was king in South Wales and the vessel's first port was Barry to load coal.

Being the youngest and nimblest, he was told to scramble ashore and make fast the stern line.

'What do I make it fast to?' he asked.

Evidently the operation was not going quite according to plan.

'Don't just **** stand there boy,' shouted the Captain. 'Tie the **** rope on to any **** thing'...which the boy did before scrambling back on board.

A few hours later, an old man on the wall, who had been sitting there quietly smoking his pipe, called down, 'Cap'n. Are ye there?'

The Captain appeared from below, where he had been having his dinner. 'Are you wantin' something, Mister?'

'Ay Cap'n,' replied the man in his singsong Welsh accent. 'If I were you Cap'n, I'd cast off this stern line here. Train's leavin' in a couple o' minutes and there's a tunnel just ahead.' • *Hugo du Plessis*

Early morning dip

We motored the Nicholson 55 into Rothesay in the Isle of Bute on a freezing March evening, and tied up to a trawler moored alongside the high harbour wall. On the jetty, parked cars were universally white under a rime of hard ice.

Quickly we squared off the boat and went ashore for fish and chips and beer. When we returned later, we were breathing out clouds of steam in the clear night air. We squeezed into our sleeping bags wearing many extra layers. I was up forward on the sailbags.

The combination of beer and freezing cold took its natural course and at 0500 I reluctantly climbed out of my bag, put on my boots and, not wanting to disturb my friends, squeezed out of the forehatch like the Michelin Man.

The next operation involved standing up and using both hands, breaking the old sailing ship rule of one hand for the ship and one for oneself. Standing up was relatively simple, but during the subsequent manoeuvre I slipped on the ice, was tripped neatly by the guardrails and fell cleanly over the side.

It would be fair to say that the water was cold. Also it was pitch dark. Never mind. I could rely on my nine friends.

Not a bit of it. Despite my cries they slept on and on. I swam around the boat, banging hard on the hull—it was like banging on the hull of the QE2—all to no avail.

Quite properly, there were no Irish pennants hanging down and the trawler masked the jetty ladder. Shedding my boots, I considered swimming across the harbour to look for another ladder, but I hadn't been to Rothesay before and there didn't seem to be too much time for a hydrographic survey.

Between the two boats a spring hung tantalisingly out of reach. Remembering the antics of the porpoises in Marine World, I swam downwards as far as possible, then upwards and out through the surface like a reluctant Polaris missile, reaching for the spring. I missed. Successive abortive attempts concentrated the mind somewhat, but eventually first one hand then two grasped the rope.

I can hardly credit now that I managed to work upwards towards the guardrails and then on to the high freeboard of the Nicholson 55, more than fully clothed. I was younger then.

In the morning, I did not ask the crew if they had slept well. It seemed to me that their amusement at the solid iced block of clothes on the deck was somewhat insensitive. • *Mike Cudmore*

Flying mice on the Deben

Not all sailing hazards take place on the high seas. My lovely Boston smack, *Rhoda*, home to myself and large black cat Kizzy, spends most of the year securely nestled in good Deben mud. Nights are peaceful, with the occasional cry of a curlew or the nocturnal comings and goings of my feline companion.

One night, Kizzy had a particularly successful time, and in a generous mood, jumped on to my bed to present her gift—a decapitated mouse. I was unimpressed, but, not wanting to hurt her feelings, I simply wrapped the corpse in kitchen paper, lobbed it out of the hatch and went back to sleep.

Before that day there had never been a boat moored alongside mine. There are always free berths in the boatyard and, coming home late, I hadn't noticed the large red sloop, tied alongside *Rhoda* for the night, prevented from reaching her own berth by the ever-encroaching mud. And it was truly unfortunate that the hurriedly thrown mouse descended with deadly accuracy through the open forehatch of my new neighbour. If I had stood on the deck and aimed deliberately at the narrow hatch, I would have missed every time.

The following day, the boatyard owner, between paroxysms of laughter, told me that the mouse had woken the sleeping sloop's occupants by landing on the pillow between them. As flying decapitated mice are not a normal hazard of peaceful marina berths, they had gone straight to him, the owner, first thing in the morning. I braced myself to go and apologise...after all, I could hardly blame the cat, could I?

• *Vanessa Rawlings*

Moon River

It was a beautiful sunny morning with a gentle breeze off the land as we beat up the channel between the mudflats. We were myself and *Rougelle*, a Deben six-tonner, which was home as I explored the shallow creeks of the Chesapeake Bay on America's Eastern Seaboard.

We'd reached the entrance to Onancock Creek the evening before, anchored for the night and set off after breakfast to sail the four miles up to Fred's house. Waiting there should be some engine spares. Until then, we sailed.

With every tack, I pushed a bit further to the edge of the channel, as one does, until the inevitable happened and we went aground.

It was just after low water, but it was apparent that we'd sailed up a slight trench. With a tidal range of about a foot, we would be there for a while.

After a month moving up the shallow waters of the Intracoastal Waterway, I had routines for getting off in a hurry (involving lots of messing about in the rubber dinghy), and a more relaxed version for when there was no time problem and it was a nice place—like now.

I threw the kedge over the stern on chain and a nylon warp

and wound it tight on the windlass, to let the spring in the nylon keep the tension. Then I ran around the deck a bit to try to rock her off, failed, and so hung a couple of five-gallon water containers from the boom end and swung out with them, leaning over the boom in the hope that the heel would release the keel. No luck, so I settled down to wait for the tide.

There was no hurry. The surroundings were beautiful, the day warm and life was good. I put on my old cut-off jeans (a washed-out pink memory of a seventies' adolescence), had a swim in the 4ft 6in depth and gave it an hour before trying again.

As I got organised, a multi-storey American powerboat came past. Seeing my predicament, her owner turned and radioed to ask if I'd like him to come past slowly to make a good wash to try to bounce her off. I thanked him, and waved gratitude to him, his friend and their wives. They waved back, pointed at my red ensign and generally made 'Welcome to the USA' gestures, looking at us through binoculars and telephoto lenses.

They started their run. As they came past, I swung out again, leaning over the boom, back toward my benefactors.

Rougelle lifted, jerked, and I started to slip off the boom, grabbing the topping lift to secure myself. It's a shame that I didn't have my hands free, since my jeans chose that moment to fall down, leaving me mooning at my helpers.

I felt very ungrateful, and, even worse, unaesthetic, as my pink jeans clashed horribly with my blushing cheeks!

And, of course, we didn't get off. Funnily enough, my American friends didn't offer to try again—there's only so far anyone will go to make a visitor welcome! • *Jonno Barrett*

Mutiny on the Orwell

Even on a calm, sunny day, isn't it amazing how problems can arise and how one problem can so easily lead to another?

We were tacking up from Harwich to Pin Mill when our fine yacht, *Firefly*, came to a shuddering halt. The skipper—a Captain Bligh type—promptly ordered his first mate into the water to apply his shoulder to the hull and, with his effort and some engine assistance, we began to move off.

Then, suddenly, the engine coughed, spluttered and died.

Apparently the dinghy painter had slackened off and become entangled with the prop. The mate received the new order to disentangle the recalcitrant rope. Minutes later he emerged from the depths with a severed end, and it was then that we saw the dinghy, freed from its tether, bobbing along on the tide towards Harwich.

Now thoroughly exasperated, the skipper barked a further instruction to his mate to recover it. But, like Mr Christian, this worthy had had enough. He mutinied. So, muttering threats of retribution, the skipper hastily stripped to the buff, plunged in and set of in hot pursuit.

A powerful swimmer, he reached the dinghy clambered aboard, carefully avoiding the rowlocks, and started back. Then a new situation arose in the shape of a large cargo vessel which seemed to have our boat clearly in its sights. To make matters worse, a gust of wind caught the sails and we began to move off!

So there we were, nude skipper rowing frantically against the tide to assume command, his mate still sulkily immersed in the muddy water, and two inexperienced females, sailing away!

Of course, there was a happy ending. The skipper arrived back in the nick of time and we suffered no more than a buffeting in the cargo vessel's wake. The mate buried his head in the booze locker, the skipper covered his 'embarrassment' and my friend and I resumed our sunbathing. • *Maureen Lever*

Soul 'bearing'

I have one irrational fear concerning my boat: dismantling the winches—a fear which comes from my ignorance of what is inside the drums. I used to be convinced that all the five-million components would leap out if I took them apart.

Last season in Greece, where we keep our boat, my wife was complaining about grease oozing from the top of one of the winches, following their last service.

We were anchored in Nidri bay, near the ferry docks, and gingerly, I began to lift off the drum of the offending winch. My wife was poised to assist if things got out of hand. The drum lifted easily to expose first one set of roller bearings and then two. Finally the drum was free from the spindle and I was in total control of it—until something fell.

I just managed to glimpse the third roller bounce on the sidedeck and drop overboard. It had stayed lurking in the drum, planning its escape. I quickly went forward to get an anchor buoy, tied it to something weighty, and threw it over to mark the spot as the boat swung. The water was too deep for me to dive, but I knew someone with an aqualung.

However, when I tracked him down, he explained that the silt stirred up by the local ferries not only reduced underwater visibility but also allowed small and heavy objects to sink into it. The possibility of finding our make of winch spares in Levkas did not exist.

I went in search of a magnet which my wife then trawled over the locality for an hour or so in the dinghy. Then I had a go—for several hours—without success.

Some months later at the Boat Show, I bought a replacement bearing. Passing back through the stands and on my way out, I spotted a 'Sea Search' magnet on a stall.

'Look!' I said exasperatedly to my wife, 'This would have picked it up, no problem.' Wrong! The bearing was non-magnetic. • *Trevor Doran*

Own goal

Evening was approaching and, after enjoying some of Fiji's best scuba-diving, it was time to make for a safe anchorage. Earlier we had set the fisherman anchor of our 40ft ketch on the top of a coral head and now we motored forward slowly hoping to lift it quickly. However, it resisted all the crew's efforts, so the anchor warp, which was made of polypropylene and floated, was thrown overboard to mark the spot where we could recover the entire ground tackle the following day.

We set off for the nearby island of Namara but, almost immediately, there was a shout from the deck. The anchor warp was following. The engine was disengaged and the lightest member of our party quickly donned her face mask. We hung her over the starboard side by her feet so she could view the situation.

Apparently, in attempting to raise the anchor, the boat had come into contact with it and a fluke had penetrated the hull, so that the ground tackle was now attached to a 'midships point of the hull.

The crew recovered the warp, while I dashed below to seek the intruding anchor fluke. I found it protruding, together with a jet of sea water, in an accessible locker. Armed with a hammer and sundry emergency materials, I knocked the fluke back through the hull and plugged the hole with a wooden bung and an old shirt. The leak was not completely stopped, but at least it could be contained by the automatic bilge pump until we reached the safety of our anchorage, where we made a more permanent repair the next day. • *E F Dowdall*

Self-launching

The season's first launching is, for me, a most stressful time—an anxiety which dates back to my first boat, over 10 years ago.

My dad and I were standing at the bottom of the slip at Gosport with *Y-Draig*, my newly-built 19ft Newbridge Navigator, perched on a small, purpose-built launching trolley. This sat upon a car trailer which, in turn, was hitched to the back of a Ford Transit. The whole outfit had been reversed down, ready for the launch.

The plan was that we would lever the launching trolley down the trailer, whereupon gravity would take over and the boat would roll smartly into the sea.

The tide began to lap at the concrete, beckoning the boat into the water, and we started to lever the trolley down the trailer. We inched it carefully past the axle.

'Look out!' somebody shouted, as the truck started to roll toward the sea.

It may be obvious to some, but it wasn't to us, that, as the weight of the boat went past the rear of the axle, it pressed the back of the trailer down. This lifted the front of the trailer, and the truck's rear wheels, rendering the parking brake useless.

I sprinted for the cab and stamped my foot hard on the brake pedal. By this time, however, we had gathered considerable momentum and my efforts had little effect: the boat continued to travel in the same direction and at virtually the same speed.

Y-Draig shot straight off the end of the trailer and flew for about five feet before landing in the water. Had it not been for my father's presence of mind in grabbing a mooring warp, she would have carried on. I would perhaps have been the only person to have built, launched and lost a boat, without having even set foot upon her. • *Mark Crew*

Flying tackle

What do a chef, a tank commander and a submariner have in common? Answer, we were three potential Day Skippers being pounded badly on Bembridge Bank. Together with our valiant instructor and courtesy of the Joint Services Sailing Centre, the four of us had enjoyed a marvellous week in the Solent with our 27ft Halcyon.

When we hit, we hit hard.

'You—start the engine. You two get the sails off her!' The sails came down but the engine wouldn't start. We discovered later that it chose this precise moment to drop a valve.

We dropped the anchor to prevent us from being dragged further up the bank. Then the pounding started and we lost the rudder. The pilot of a Hovercraft used his fans to try and blow us out of danger, but to no avail and he left us to our plight.

'Get the kedge out,' I heard someone say.

'Where is it?'

'It's in the forepeak—come on—move!'

I took it upon myself to fetch it. The saloon was a shambles. I remember having to crawl, as it was impossible to stay upright. I recall the damage the anchor did to the furniture as I battled my way back to the saloon. But what I really cringe at is what happened next.

From the saloon I threw the kedge and warp up through the companionway to the guy in the cockpit. 'Get the kedge over the side,' I heard as it was in mid-air.

The lad in the cockpit must have been a rugby player. He received the kedge perfectly, spun around and passed the whole lot overboard! Yes, anchor warp, the lot, went over the side.

Stunned silence. I looked at him, he looked at me, we looked at the instructor. Hanging on to the backstay with an expression of total defeat on his face he uttered his immortal words.

'I've been sailing since I was seven but I have never, ever seen anything like that before.' • *Haydn Windle*

Where angels fear to tread

It was our first major voyage in our 26ft Westerly Centaur. My husband Ian, our three young sons and I had been stormbound for four days off Lundy Island in the Bristol Channel, and had arrived in Saundersfoot Harbour at 0300 after a rough crossing in bad seas and fog.

So far, with children being seasick, halyards lost around rigging, engine failure and rocks, the maiden voyage had been eventful. We settled down for some sleep.

Next morning we set sail for Swansea, the family exhausted from the previous day. I felt confident enough to helm across the bay by myself, so I sent Ian below to get some rest with the children. I sailed to the sound of quiet snoring below.

Looking at the chart for the northern end of Carmarthen Bay, it seemed that the passage between Worms Head Island and the mainland would shorten the journey. The chart gave depths of 13ft. Further on, however, I started to get the nagging feeling that things were not all as they seemed, and woke my grumbling husband to check the chart. As he appeared from below and examained the chart his sleep-filled face changed to one of amazement. 'You have checked the chart haven't you?' he asked in a slightly suspicious voice.

'Yes, of course,' I replied. 'It shows 13ft depth.'

Ian checked the echo sounder, which read 13ft, and took the helm. The depth readings started to drop with alarming rapidity. People were running along the clifftop and as Ian pointed out, 'Nobody runs to witness good seamanship...but rather to see an idiot pile his boat up on to the rocks.'

The echo sounder now read 3ft 6in and we draw 3ft 3in. With bated breath we scraped across. Grabbing the chart, Ian pointed to the black line beneath the 13ft.

'It means 13ft above sea level, not below,' he said, adding a passing reference to a foolish bovine...

On one of the highest tides of the year I had navigated our boat over a causeway that spends most of the year above water. Had we touched down, we would have been unable to get off for at least three months. • *Bette Blayney*

PEYTON

Blame the ship's cat

If a pet is to become part of a sailing household, it deserves a go at the family's weekend fun. The day came when our cat, Teddy, a short-haired British Blue, was invited to sail aboard *Oosik*, our Ericson 32. All was well at first, but eventually Teddy succumbed to the gentle Pacific swells and brought up his most recent dinner, all over everything. I headed home quickly and, having berthed, my wife, Debbie, scooped up the unfortunate cat and carried him to the more stable pontoon.

I set about attacking the mess and went below carrying with me the water hose from the pontoon. I was busy with the washing down when I heard a loud scream from Debbie and arrived up on deck to find her badly scratched by the still frightened animal. After calming them both down and tending to Deb's wounds, I felt it best to get them both home.

Several hours later, I received a call from the club's berthing master to say that a curious thing had happened to my boat. He had found her with just inches of freeboard, hanging by her lines, and completely full of fresh water. A running hose was also found heading down the companionway. Auxiliary pumps were handling the water but 'did I have any insight into the problem?'

A very embarrassed skipper sped back to the club. • *John A Blum*

Repel boarders!

We were anchored in a tiny cove off Culebra's Ensenada Honda, recovering from our windward slog along the south coast of Puerto Rico. It was Sunday morning, and we were lounging in the cockpit, noses poked into paperback novels, when the drone of an approaching outboard motor caught my attention. I suggested to Carol that we should put on some clothes.

A small motor-boat with a Bimini top was heading towards us. Aboard were two men in dark suits and a lady dressed for a garden party. The lady was kneeling on the small seat in the bow, struggling to keep her balance and holding a tabloid newspaper aloft.

As they drew closer, I could see that the newspaper was *The Watchtower* and realised that the trio were waterborne Jehovah's Witnesses.

I waved them off before they could come alongside, assuming from their non-nautical appearance that their boat-handling skills were minimal and afraid that, if they dinged *Adriana*'s topsides, I would say something which would condemn my soul to eternal damnation.

Carol emerged from the cabin, having donned T-shirt and shorts, to express the opinion that our visitors' sudden about-turn had less to do with my imperious arm-waving than with my failure to follow my own advice and put on my pants. • *John Schofield*

A cardinal sin

We were on passage from St Vaast-la-Hougue to Ouistreham, a small port on the Normandy coast of France. It was late in the day and the light was beginning to fade. As we approached our destination our estimated position was proving difficult to confirm with a fix. There were no clearly identifiable features on the coast and it was too early for lights to be of help.

As the coastline closed, the relaxed atmosphere aboard drifted gradually into apprehension. According to the chart, the area was littered with wrecks, visible at chart datum, and a falling tide did little to inspire confidence. If only we could spot the north cardinal that would enable us to make a safe approach. I scanned the horizon with the binoculars as the depth decreased inexorably.

Nothing.

Suddenly, out of the gloom, I spotted it; the unmistakable yellow with black-upward-pointing cone. A quick bearing and check on the chart confirmed that we could steer safely for the north cardinal and then make our approach to Ouistreham.

Spirits rose as we altered course, confident in the knowledge that we would make a safe entrance before nightfall. Thoughts now turned to an evening of fun ashore, with plenty of time to find a restaurant for drinks and a meal. Fifteen minutes later, the cardinal was clearly visible. A quick check with the binoculars.

It's amazing how instantly the morale of the crew can change on a yacht, particularly for the worse.

It is clear to me that there is a need for an amendment to the Collision Regulations and that the new clause should read something like: 'A fisherman will not be permitted to fish alone in a small yellow inflatable dinghy whilst wearing yellow oilskins and a pointed black hat within a 20-mile radius of a north cardinal mark.'

The navigator was in a bad mood for the rest of the day. • *Mike Streets*

Adrift?

It was back in the '60s when, in a Trintella 30, we dropped anchor for the night in Newtown, Isle of Wight, with several other yachts along the reach leading to Clamerkin Lake. It was Springs.

Four of us had returned from the Shalfleet pub in the Avon dinghy after closing time, singing 'Nellie Dean' loudly enough for the beautiful harmonies to be appreciated above the noise of the outboard and finally we all turned in.

Suddenly there was a crash, followed by a dramatic cry of, 'All hands on deck!' There was a yacht against our starboard side and our skipper was shining a torch into her cabin windows and shouting 'You're adrift!'

We pushed the boat clear as the owner surfaced and watched her as she disappeared towards the harbour entrance.

Still half asleep, we were horrified when there was another crash—this time on our port quarter—once again followed by Skip thumping on their coachroof, shining his torch and shouting, 'You're adrift!'

It took another similar collision and more cries of 'You're adrift!' before Bob, who had been anchorman when we arrived, suddenly dashed to the foredeck and laid out a further 3 or 4 fathoms of chain. Then everything went quiet and the realisation hit us. It was us who had dragged through the fleet creating mayhem.

All was now peaceful on the mooring, except for the bad tempered shouting and cursing from the boats that we had just left. We stood silently in our darkened cockpit, until eventually

their lights went out and we returned thoughtfully to our bunks.
As we went below the skipper asked, 'What time's first light?'
'Five o'clock, Skip.'
'We'll leave at four thirty,' he said. • *Reg Melhuish*

Deathraft

We busied ourselves with final preparations for departure from
Brighton. John was on deck tweaking the rigging. Tony was
clearing the breakfast. I had drawn the short straw and was
washing up. Owner/skipper Bill went aft into the quarterberth to
fetch the liferaft to be secured on deck.

A moment later, he emerged, struggling with the bright-orange
valise which contained the six-man liferaft. There was a loud
bang, followed by a very loud hiss and Bill's scream of 'Bloody
Hell, look out!' I was knocked on to the cabin sole as a pair of
size-11 seaboots stomped over me.

I rose to be pushed back and almost engulfed by a black
monster which was growing before me. The port-side locker
cracked loudly as the timbers shattered. The engine box, which
also formed the bottom steps of the companionway, split and
broke away. Still the hissing continued and still the black mass
expanded.

By now I was pinned with my back to the sink.

'Stab the bloody thing!' a voice behind me screamed. I reached
into the sink and grabbed at the cutlery. My fingers closed on a
knife and I stabbed at the blackness that was gripping me. My
arm bounced back, wrenching my shoulder muscles and
inflicting as much damage to the liferaft as a toddler on a bouncy
castle. You cannot kill an inflating liferaft with a buttered butter
knife.

Over my shoulder other arms and hands, holding blades,
swished and slashed through the fabric. With a great 'whoosh!'
the black frightener collapsed, only to grow again as the next
compartment began to inflate.

More slashing and stabbing and down it went again.

'Get it out,' yelled Tony.

We grabbed at the lacerated strips of fabric and threw it,
inclusive of the attached gas bottle, into the cockpit. Running up

the companionway, we stood staring at the quivering remains.

Not a word was spoken, but the decision was unanimous—the three of us reached down and threw the lot over the side. It landed on the pontoon with a crash. 'What did you do that for?' asked a bemused John from the foredeck, oblivious of the recently averted catastrophe. It was the flash of sunlight reflecting on the shiny blade still gripped in the skipper's hand that silenced further comment.

The entire incident took less than one minute. The memory will last rather longer. • *C D Boswell-Williams*

Help!

I had to get my newly-purchased Sabre 27 into the water quickly, step the mast, and commission her in time for next weekend. It was the start of the Whitbread Round the World Race and we could not miss that.

I had watched the start of the previous race from my friend's Rival 32 and noticed that, in the chaos, the skipper had seen nothing of the excitement. He spent all his time avoiding other boats. But, my goodness, it was exciting. I had to be there for this one...*never* was a boat more hurriedly, or thoughtlessly, commissioned.

My plan was good: stay away from the start, sail quietly over to Whitecliffe Bay, drop the hook, enjoy a languid lunch, then amble over to Bembridge Ledge buoy and watch the fun. Things went well. Only about twenty boats had the same idea. Lunch over, we got the anchor up and sailed to the buoy. There were a few more boats around now, but it was still not crowded. Think of those poor mugs bouncing around off Gilkicker, ho ho!

My crew was Ann, a wife who had just found out, after 18 years, that she liked sailing after all, hence the Sabre in lieu of my previous Achilles 24.

Then I saw the white maelstrom coming at me like a charging herd of buffalo.

Don't panic, I thought. 'What did you say?' said Ann.

'Nothing, we'll be all right.'

'Why did you say that?'

Casually, I dropped the main and roller-reefed the genoa, started the Yanmar 12 and pointed the boat in the direction of the herd's likely course.

They hit us a few minutes later, and it was wild, mad, exciting, scary and a lot of fun. The seas were crazy; we were semi-pooped a couple of times, brushed aside by ferries determined to give their paying clients a good view. The seamanship book was thrown out of the window. I had a maniacal grin on my face as Dennis Conner passed me 30ft away. He didn't wave. Ann was white-knuckling the backstay with one hand and shooting photos with the other.

At the height of my bliss, with still a third of the fleet to come, and surrounded by Whitbread boats sailing at 14 knots, the tiller came off in my hand. The bolt clamping it to the bracket must have been loose. It hadn't been checked.

Boats missed me by inches. We were going in semi-circles and I was on my knees trying to fit a one-inch rod into a one-inch-and-a-whisker hole, all the time sitting on a bucking bronco.

Glancing up, I saw a Whitbread yacht coming straight at me, 50ft away, with big lads screaming at me to move my boat. I couldn't quite catch the exact words due to the wind, but Ann's ears were red from the cold. You don't read boat names in that position, but they were wearing blue-and-yellow oilies.

I stood up quickly, waved the tiller frantically over my head and screamed that I was out of control. They had to luff right up to miss me. Ann stuffed the camera down her jacket and was now as one with the backstay, knuckles glistening, and semi-praying the helpful comment, 'Get us out of here, Pete!'

At that moment, the tiller clunked on to the bracket, albeit pointing through the pushpit, and I steered out of trouble to effect repairs in calmer waters. • *Peter Webb*

Black mark

Some years ago, we kept a Heavenly Twins catamaran in Brittany. With four young children, all under the age of 10, packing for a three-week summer holiday was both an art and a science. Our method was to load everything into black plastic bin bags.

With everyone sitting in his or her allotted seat in the car, the bin bags were then packed tightly in and around everyone in our modestly sized seven-seater. It was very successful; the soft bags were ideal for dozing against and had the security of a permanent air bag! When we arrived on board, everything would be unpacked with nothing to show but a small roll of black plastic bags ready for the return journey.

The summer of 1989 was very, very hot in northern France. As we rolled off the Cherbourg ferry and migrated south, a strong, pungent, but unidentified smell began to engulf the

car. Casual comments were passed over the standard of hygiene of various members of the family, not to mention the age of their socks. At times, the accusations became really quite personal. Suspicion passed to our two-year old and the state of his nappy; a lay-by and a detailed inspection again drew a blank. The last two hours of a very long journey resulted in an offended silence all round.

It was not until we unpacked in the boat that we realised I had inadvertently packed three bags in the car which my wife had put out for the rubbish collection. • *Peter Firstbrook*

Rum flambé

We were resting one dark Caribbean evening at Leverick Bay, Virgin Gorda, in the British Virgin Islands. After a few Pussers' rums, we felt it seamanlike to leave an anchor light so that we would be able to find *Bellamanda*, our Bowman 40, after a few more painkillers ashore at Pussers' Inn.

Leaving the Tilley lamp hanging under the bimini top, I felt a little uneasy as the boat rocked gently in the swell but, having left her like this many times before, why should we worry?

As we arrived at the dinghy dock with our friends, we took a last look out into the bay to check our bearings for the more hazardous return trip.

Panic! *Bellamanda*'s stern was engulfed in flames. The Tilley lamp must have slid down the bimini top and smashed into the cockpit, spilling paraffin.

We leapt into the dinghy and after a Le Mans-type start we set off, flat out (well, 4hp flat out), only to come to an immediate standstill. The only stray line off the pontoon had wound itself around our propeller—the last thing we needed.

Off again, brain in overdrive—where were those fire extinguishers? How much damage would there be? Could we continue our cruise or would we be going home in just our shorts and tee-shirts?

As we rounded the outer dock, the truth dawned. There was *Bellamanda* with her Tilley light twinkling and, one boat further along, a fine blazing barbecue! • *Alan J Taylor*

Break-in and entry

We had moored up on an outside trot in the Tamar River and rowed ashore to spend the evening with friends. A couple of hours later we returned to find the dinghy, but no sign of the boat. Thick fog had descended and, to make matters worse, the tide was now screaming down river.

We decided we were strong and fit, so I began to row frantically and just managed to stem the stream. We saw a yacht and my wife managed to grab at the topsides. I relaxed, somewhat breathless, and released the oars to help her, as her arms were being pulled out of their sockets. Immediately one of the oars was flipped out of its rowlock, leaving us clinging to a small sailing boat with no adequate means of further propulsion against the tide.

By this time, the fog had thickened and we could now see neither our boat nor the shore. There was no way back and no way forward until the stream lessened. We tied on, and sat and thought; then we climbed aboard and sat and got damp and cold. It was midnight and there were still three or four hours to go before there was any chance of the stream slackening sufficiently.

We made a decision. We broke into the cabin. It was my first and only break-in and entry. I have to say it needed only a gentle pull on the padlock but we felt very guilty. Below it was dry with two berths and even two blankets.

Four hours later we awoke to absolute stillness. No wind. No current. And we could see our boat. We sculled over to her as quickly as we could, climbed aboard and motored off before anyone could say 'boo'. We had left a short note of apology written in my wife's lipstick, and all the money we had (£3) to pay for the repair to the lock.

To the owner of our shelter that night, whoever he or she might be, thank you and our sincere apologies for the damaged lock. • *Alan Lloyd-Edwards*

Special recipe

After a relatively fast 30-mile passage from the Jakarta port of Tanjong Priok, it was a pleasure to drop anchor at last at Palau Sepa in the Thousand Islands. The afternoon brought balmy conditions and *Moby Dick*, our 33ft steel sloop, lay peacefully at anchor. With our two daughters and family visitors from the UK on board, the order of the day was 'Get the Tinker out and explore'.

A double helping of two-stroke oil into the only petrol on board soon brought about the temporary demise of the outboard and it was too hot to row far! 'Not to worry. I'm sure they have petrol on the island.' And, sure enough, within half an hour peace returned as the children motored off to explore the fabulous snorkelling spots.

Meanwhile adult thoughts turned to G&Ts and preparation for the evening meal. As dusk fell, the kids returned to the fold.

The many advantages of a portable LPG stove were now evident as Thérèse cooked in the after end of *Moby*'s long cockpit. It didn't matter that the light was up forward being used for reading. Everything was ready.

'Hold it, I smell gas,' cried Thérèse. When island cruising, we simply strap the gas cylinder to the after rail and cook only in the cockpit so that no leak can find its way below. A quick but thorough search failed to find any sign of a leak; there were no suspicious hisses from the cooker or bottles.

It must be imagination, we thought. But again, when the cook re-started, there was, indeed, a strong smell of gas. Saucepan in hand this time, she stated more forcefully that there was a gas leak. Only as the pan descended towards the flame did the horrified crew realise that it was not water the cabbage was being cooked in...

The petrol from the island had been delivered in a used bottle identical to those we use for our own water supply.

Since then we have had our own steel petrol can and cabbage has never tasted the same.

• *Richard Lamble*

Bitter experience

It was our first sail in our recently-acquired 30-footer. The crew, my wife Anne and our three young children, had watched impatiently as I started to paint depth markings on the anchor chain and, so, being as anxious as they were to cast off, I abandoned the task and we headed for Rothesay Bay to have lunch at anchor.

It was a beautiful spring day and, as we approached the anchorage opposite the Skeoch Wood, I saw that it was very busy with several boats already moored there. I got the sails down and motored in to anchor. I was in deeper water than I had intended and was ready to let a good length of chain run out.

As the anchor plunged to the sea-bed, the chain rattled over the roller faster and faster, more and more noisily until I virtually forgot about the many experienced eyes on me, so hypnotic was the movement and sound.

Suddenly, I was watching with horror and disbelief as the bitter end of the chain danced, almost in slow motion, over the roller and disappeared into the dark depths, with a vaguely discernible plop.

For a minute or two I was stunned but gradually I became aware of the curious stares from the surrounding boats. Panic took over. My face now scarlet, I brushed past the children who were edging along the deck to look over the side, jumped into

the cockpit beside my startled wife, who was just about to serve a meal, and threw the engine hard ahead. If I left quickly enough perhaps my fellow sailors in the bay would not remember the name of the boat with the deranged skipper who came into the anchorage at top speed, jettisoned his ground tackle and then left as quickly as he had arrived. If only I had marked the full length of chain I would have noticed that the bitter end had not been secured.

To this day my wife and my children, now grown up, still refer to Rothesay Bay as Anchor Bay. • *Robin Graham*

Chocolate soldier

The yacht was moored on the pontoon opposite the Folly Inn and we were returning from a trip ashore to Newport, Isle of Wight. The weather was sunny but cool and I was wearing my virgin red waterproofs and new sailing wellies. The tide was definitely on its way out, since the dinghy sat on the mud beside the pontoons and the bilge-keelers. The Medina was a shallow stream in the middle of the mud.

'We only need a few inches of water to float the inflatable. The stream will take us until we can get into deeper water and use the outboard,' I announced confidently.

So three piled in the dinghy and yours truly, the only wearer of wellies, dragged the dinghy across the slippery mud to the stream. It was easy but I couldn't help getting splatters of mud on my new red waterproofs.

If we had been 10 minutes sooner, I reckon that we would have made it. As it was, we moved 10 yards down stream and came to a soft halt in a couple of inches of water. No amount of paddling, pushing or rocking would move us on. The water had all but gone.

Our giggling attracted some attention as we considered the possibility of giving up and waiting for the tide. The humour of our predicament was not lost on the inhabitants of the bilge-keelers, as several faces appeared and some children pointed at four people sitting in a dinghy in the middle of the mud.

I stepped over to drag the dinghy, plus three passengers, back to the pontoon. I must have put my left foot in to a deep bit for, putting my full weight on to it, the water came in over the top of my welly.

As I felt the cool water flow in, I tried instinctively to pull my foot out of the mud. The suction was considerable and I only succeeded in lifting my left foot clean out of the welly. Inevitably I overbalanced. I put out a hand to save myself (and especially my waterproofs) from the fall. My hand disappeared into the soft mud which oozed horribly up the inside of my sleeve.

If the laughter was loud now, it got louder as I rolled slowly and irresistibly backwards, falling on my elbow and sitting down firmly in the mud. Whereas before I was mainly red, now I was mostly brown. The laughter got still louder as I had to re-insert my soggy foot into the small round hole in the mud—now filled with brown water—in order to retrieve my left welly.

No point worrying about credibility now. I was covered in it. As I dragged the dinghy, with three hysterical people back to the pontoon, past the smug bilge-keelers and tittering spectators, I made a point of sharing my credibility with anyone in splattering range. • *Lec Zylko*

Brixham tea party

It was our first season with our first cruiser and we were still on the steep part of the learning curve. Towards the end of a lazy day's sail in Torbay, we were approaching the sailing club floating pontoons at Brixham to tie up for the night.

Anyone using these pontoons, which are held in place by chains and anchors, should be aware, as we were, that your performance in mooring up is in full view of the clubhouse immediately above and is likely to be the subject of critical discussion. Consequently, we were all set to put on a good show.

Approaching, we could see that, on the far side of the pontoon we were heading for, the occupants of a smart yacht were taking tea in the afternoon sunshine, sitting quietly at their cockpit table and enjoying the peace.

All went well at first and Sue jumped ashore promptly with the bow line; I followed with the stern line after slowing down with a touch astern. Once on the pontoon I found, to my horror, that the boat was not stopping...I had returned the throttle to slow forward gear. I was amazed at the power that was exerted and, as the line ran through my fingers, I just managed to get it around the pontoon cleat before the boat sailed away.

However, it now proceeded to tow the pontoon to the limit of its mooring chains along with the attached yacht. By the time I had managed to leap back aboard and return the throttle to neutral the tea party had been well and truly disrupted as our neighbours found themselves being dragged across the harbour. But now, with the tension off, the whole assembly suddenly changed direction and lurched back again, sending teacups crashing before coming gradually to a stop.

My apology was met by a stony silence, and we retreated below, away from the glares across the pontoon and the watching eyes from the clubhouse above. • *David M Thorne*

Hanging around in the Hamble

My story occurred in March. It was a Saturday and we had just finished our race training. Sunday was to be another race in the Warsash Spring Series. It was raining heavily and blowing hard as we came into the marina. As soon as we tied up everyone leapt ashore to run to the bar for food, warmth and a drink. I dithered a little and, when I emerged from below, the pontoon was deserted.

In my haste to catch up, I grabbed a team oilskin jacket to keep me dry. The jacket was much too large for me and the zip did not seem to work. I hastily fastened the Velcro and left it at that before hurrying out on deck. The wind was still howling and the yacht was being blown off the pontoon. There was a 3ft gap between the hull and the walkway. I did what I had done many times before; I stepped over the guardrails, and jumped. The coat tails of the jacket caught on one of the stanchions, and there I was, suspended by my coat, with my feet 18in above the water

and the pontoon completely out of reach. After what seemed like hours, the Velcro gave way.

Spadoosh! Straight down the gap! The whole farce happened in slow motion which gave me plenty of time to contemplate the inevitable. The water closed above my head before I bobbed back up gasping at the ice-cold of the Hamble.

I hung to the pontoon with my arms, feet flailing underneath, but I could find no foothold. I crabbed my way along the float until I got to the boat's taut bow rope which I managed to get my leg over and I scrambled on to the pontoon.

When, eventually, I made it to the bar, after a shower and a change, nobody believed my story...until I wrung out my money on the table! • *Liz King*

Surprise catch

It was a lovely summer's evening, and Joyce and I were sitting in the cockpit of our 28ft sloop *Endil* enjoying a gin and tonic before supper.

We were on our mooring buoy in Salcott Creek, West Mersea, and the tide was chuckling along, almost at full flood. Suddenly I noticed, in the middle of the creek, a white fender floating towards us.

As it came nearer, I saw that it was a small white buoy and that it had writing on it. Reading it upside-down it said 'Down River'. I assumed that it was from one of the lobster pots or long lines often seen in the mouth of the River Blackwater. As it drifted closer, I called to Joyce to pass me the boathook and, leaning over, hooked it aboard. As I did so, I saw that it had a long line attached and I felt a tug.

I shouted to Joyce, 'We've caught something. Quick, help me pull it up.'

Joyce grabbed the line and as she did so there was an even heavier tug. 'That's not a lobster pot,' said Joyce, 'it feels too heavy. It could be a seal has got tangled up in it.'

Together we hauled the line aboard over the pushpit, with tugs on the line becoming even more violent. We were becoming very excited by now and the crew of a nearby boat were cheering our efforts to land our catch.

Suddenly, to our utter shock and amazement, in a foam of bubbles, the heads of two helmeted and masked scuba divers appeared under our stern.

Our catch was a trainee scuba diver and her experienced father. It was then that I took a long look at the white buoy I had first hauled aboard and saw that the writing did not say 'Down River' but the more precise 'Diver Down'. • *Derek Wyatt*

Black hole

I was thrilled to be asked by a friend to join him on his Dehler 34 for the Round the Island Race. We were to leave London on Friday evening, sleep on board at Lymington Marina, and rise at 0500 to be race-ready at Cowes for the early starting guns. The

skipper would truck no tardiness in his keenness to be on time for the race and to have time to practise the start.

He was a popular captain and a good planner but had overdone his crew invitations, so that in the end there were seven of us and berths for only six. He slept in the back of his Volvo.

It was a pitch-black evening and all that could be seen amid the chaos below were pale white faces and sleeping bags. At 0500 we all rose promptly. I slipped on some clothes and leapt ashore for the warmth and safety of the marina facilities.

I returned 15 minutes later to find a black hole in the water where the boat had been safely moored...unbeknown to me, the skipper left his Volvo and returned to the boat in keen anticipation of a quick start.

I had no boat, no friends, no money and only a toothbrush to keep me company. Should I return to London somehow, or should I wait forlornly on the dockside? I chose to wait. Three-quarters of an hour later the boat returned and I was told, not too politely, to make it snappy and get aboard.

They had only noticed I was missing when they'd started up the channel and could not understand why I had not drunk my cup of tea. • *Rodney W Fetzer*

Ah yes, the bucket ...

One undoubted advantage of cruising in very small sailing boats
is the high 'excitement per mile' quotient sometimes experienced
when compared with bigger, faster and more stable craft. Little
did we guess, however, as we set off 'en famille' in our Drascombe
Lugger from Woodbridge, what the immediate future had in store.

Our destination was the popular anchorage at The Rocks, just a
few miles down the Deben between Waldringfield and Ramsholt.
Wafting downriver with the tide under us, I was deep in a
pleasant reverie about whether the Pools win would involve
buying the Swan right away, or maybe an interim Vancouver 34,
when my wife noticed that the occupants of a tidebound dinghy
were waving, shouting and pointing to something astern of us.

On looking back to see which item of our equipment the
children had managed to launch over the side, we were amazed
to see that we had unwittingly sailed straight past a substantial
maritime disaster. A swamped wooden dayboat of around 20ft
lay, gunwales under, in mid-river. Attached to it was a capsized
GRP dinghy. Clinging to the foundered craft were six people, and
the whole ensemble was surrounded by a slick of oars,

floorboards, wallets and other sundry flotsam, all dispersing rapidly on the tide. There was not a lifejacket in sight.

With the children viewing their first real glimpse of maritime adversity, we began hauling the bedraggled survivors aboard one by one. They were in poor shape, and I was musing on the serious effect of exhaustion and hypothermia, when my wife pointed out that they were all roaring drunk!

It transpired that a very good lunch had been enjoyed at Ramsholt and, amidst subsequent high jinks, they had somehow capsized and swamped the dayboat. Efforts to climb out and aboard the dinghy had capsized that too. Their 'game plan' at that point was to wait until the tide took them near a bank, and scramble ashore. It would have been a long wait, as their anchor had gone overboard and was pinning them in mid-river.

With the chastened and shivering youths delivered ashore to the grim-faced group of parents who by this time had gathered, we went back to try and tow in the swamped boats. We baled the dinghy with our bucket, and just managed to beach her. Then we said farewell to the shipwrecked mariners (a process involving many a clammy embrace, wringing handshake and drink-fuelled expression of gratitude), and we set off for our overnight anchorage, suffused with that rosy, self-satisfied glow that tends to accompany a deed well done.

With the cockpit tent erected, an excellent barbecue consumed, and a glorious sunset giving way to a spreading canopy of stars in the big Suffolk sky, life, we felt, had little more to offer.

In the middle of the night, our six-year old son woke up crying and proceeded to be spectacularly and violently sick. 'Quick, the bucket!' screeched his mother. Ah yes, the bucket—with a terrible flash I remembered where I had last seen it—lying in the bottom of that dinghy and now several miles away. Younger sister sat up and joined in what appeared to be a projectile vomiting competition.

Over the succeeding hours, let a veil be drawn, except to observe that, admirable as Drascombes are, they do not offer the option of a trip to the airing cupboard for a new duvet, and that there is now a salad bowl about which I shall always have ambivalent feelings. Oh yes, and we have a new ship's bucket, which is attached very securely and very permanently.

• *Mike Purves*

Entertaining Denzil

After the hottest Friday of the year, we found ourselves tied up in Ryde Marina on a grey, cold, bleak Saturday morning with a good Force 5 blowing on to the shore, and the children exchanging the preliminary insults prerequisite to a really good bust-up.

There were six of us on board our Spring 25 *Springtied*: my husband Paul, myself, three children, and Denzil, our black Labrador. Denzil, whom we acquired with sailing in mind, had been the smallest in the litter. He had since grown to the proportions of a small donkey—on a carefully balanced diet of sailing shoes (left foot only), kitchen chairs, one complete set of school books, half a No 3 jib, the *Oxford Companion to Classical Music* and a packet of wallpaper paste.

To the obvious dismay of all around us, we clambered ashore, separated the children, and despatched them to various corners of the marina to go crab fishing. Paul then felt the need come upon him, as the tide retreated, to climb into the knee-high, pungent, black mud, and scrub the slime off the boat's bottom. I went for a walk into the town.

We all returned to the boat to find a beautifully scrubbed bottom and gleaming hull. Paul returned the hose, had a shower, and retired gratefully to the cockpit opening a can of beer prior to the afternoon's siesta.

Denzil had other ideas. He had been eyeing the black slime longingly for some time and, no longer able to contain himself, he launched himself off the end of the pontoon into the mud. The resounding squelch could be heard from one end of the marina to the other.

Paul propelled himself from the cockpit and, with the aid of the boathook, retrieved Denzil before he disappeared from sight.

The dog was completely covered in thick black muck.

Denzil then did what any self-respecting Labrador would do in that situation: he shook, vigorously, coating not only our boat, but the boat opposite us, and its occupants, who were enjoying their lunch, in an even spattering of foul-smelling mud.

The mud in Ryde has a particularly tenacious quality and is not easily removed with just one shake. While being dragged up the pontoon towards the hosepipe, Denzil shook himself again and again, coating each and every single boat he passed. And, at each shake, Paul, determined not to be beaten, hurled himself upon Denzil with all the determination of a New Zealand quarter-back. Thus, man and dog walked side by side up the pontoon, both completely plastered in mud and stopped every few feet to fall to the floor in a canine half-nelson, before walking another few feet repeating the process.

We would like to take this opportunity to apologise to all who returned to their boats to find them splattered; to the people next to us who were very understanding, and even helped us scrub all the boats and the pontoon as best we could; and to the local oil refinery, which we heard receiving the blame for a fall-out of black spots. • *Susan Over*

A close attachment

At last we were sailing, after a winter of shore-based navigation evening classes. For many of us, including me, it was our first experience of a keelboat, and we were careering up and down the Orwell in a Sigma 38 in a good Force 6.

We had been introduced to the mysteries of slab-reefing and changing down the headsail, while we were all harnessed up. After a couple of hours of fun, we decided to head into Levington Marina for a break. Sails came down, fenders were put out and warps were distributed. I was put in charge of the stern line. The skipper steered into the confines of the marina.

As we came alongside, the bow man and I stepped ashore gracefully and prepared to thread the lines through the pontoon's rings. An urgent tugging at my chest revealed my mistake; my harness was still on and I was attached to the boat by an 8ft safety line. As panic swept through me, my brain seized. The bow line had been threaded and was being pulled in manfully—if it's

worth pulling in, it's worth pulling in hard. The wind, even in the shelter of the marina, was still gusting and blowing the stern out from the pontoon at a rate of knots.

In slow motion I pondered three courses of action: I could unclip the line from my harness; I could get the stern line through a ring; I could sit astride a bollard (fortunately, none was available).

By now the situation had gone from urgent to critical and I was teetering on the brink. I made a vain attempt to jump back on the boat—now some 12ft away—but only succeeded in performing a graceful leap into the uninviting waters.

My introduction to keelboats was over. • *Richard Oliver*

False (tooth) alarm

It was a fine sunny day and *Conference* was beating up the Wallet towards Harwich.

We came to the area off Walton Pier, where the only dangers for small boats are a multitude of lobster pots. Rosemary, who was at the helm at the time, suddenly felt the call of nature and vanished below.

I had just finished weaving my way through the last of the

pots when I heard a loud scream from below. Rosemary appeared on the companionway, ashen faced and tearful.

'What's happened?' I asked.

'My tooth has gone down the plughole,' she explained.

The tooth in question was a single tooth on a plate and worn at the back of the jaw. I knew that she would not rest until I found it.

I gave her the wheel and went below. She had been cleaning her teeth when the plate became dislodged and fell down the sink plughole. Unhappily for her, the sink drained directly into the sea and clearly the tooth was now resting on the bottom, if not in one of the lobster pots.

Rosemary put a brave face on the matter and, as the gap in her smile was hardly noticeable, she decided not to worry about replacing the tooth.

Two years later, we decided to take *Conference* to France. We have made the trip many times, so anticipated no problems. We left Ramsgate in a pleasant southwesterly Force 3 and ended up roaring across the Channel in a good Force 6. The sea was fairly confused and *Conference* was crashing around a lot. Rosemary struggled below to visit the heads and, when *Conference* fell into a trough, I heard a scream. I thought that she must have fallen over in the toilet compartment.

I was just about to connect the autopilot, when I heard her shout, 'I've found my tooth. What have you been playing at?'

And there she was, standing in the companionway holding the plate and tooth. She had been in the toilet compartment, had looked in the sink and found her tooth lying there.

She accused me of playing tricks, of course, but the truth is that the tooth must have become lodged in the pipework and, after two years, the crashing of the boat must have caused water to be forced up into the basin carrying the tooth with it.

Amazingly, tooth and plate were quite undamaged. She popped it into her mouth and smiled almost continuously for the rest of the cruise. • *Mervyn Beecham*

Concrete evidence

The boat was in a dark shed against a wall surrounded by junk. I said I'd like to have a look at the bottom.

'The bottom?' the owner said, cocking his head as if he had something stuck in his ear, 'the bottom?'

'Well, just a quick peep.'

He sighed, patiently. He said, 'If this was one of your wooden boats, squire, then very wise, very sensible, but this is galvanised steel. You don't get no rot and gribble or Toreador worms in your steel boats, young sir!'

It seemed reasonable. Well, you don't, do you? Anyway, I could trust him. He was, after all, an East Cowes Special Constable.

I was 17, shaving at least once a week and too tall for my trousers. 'Perhaps I can have a look down in the bilges?' I said, asserting myself.

He looked at his watch. It seemed he was expecting another 'gennelmum shortly'. An earlier viewer, it appeared, had wanted to pay cash there and then. The owner, with flattering candour, said he'd rather I had her.

I peered under floorboards.

'Concrete!' I squeaked, 'she's full of concrete!'

'Oh yes, squire, that's right, all concrete. It steadies her, concrete does.'

'But what about pumping out? Where does the bilge pump go?' I whittled.

He sighed heavily, 'She don't need no bilge pump. Now go on, arst me why she don't need no pump.'

'I arst' him why.

' 'Cause steel boats don't leak, squire,' he explained in kindly tones. 'All you need is a dustpan an' brush!'

Plainly this was the perfect boat. And in view of all those other people keen to buy, I handed over my hard-saved ten quid.

He had a receipt all ready, made out in my name. How about that for efficiency, eh?

To save me the trouble of getting her around to Wootton Creek, he even delivered her by trailer.

I put her on a mud mooring. When the tide came in she leaked like a watercart, so I hauled her out again. There must be a missing rivet somewhere. Lying underneath her I saw that the bottom paint was thick as a bachelor's pancake. With an eerie clairvoyance I rolled up my sleeve, and took a swipe with a scraper.

It want straight through the bottom. So did my fist. A gush of stinking gravy followed. • *Des Sleightholme*

Code red

We were enjoying some wonderful days sailing around the French coast and, one evening, tied up in the marina at St Servan, just opposite St Malo. Pete went to pay the mooring fees and obtain the code to enter the men's shower block. Bob and I made our way there to await him.

When Pete returned, he called, 'The Gents is closed. We can use the Ladies.'

'You're joking!'

'No, it'll be OK. I've been given the code.'

'We can't go in there.'

'Well, I am.'

He keyed in the code and peeped inside.

'It's all right. There's nobody in,' he whispered.

Three grown men crept into the Ladies, looking for all the world like three guilty schoolboys.

Three days' beard went in a matter of seconds to be replaced by 1,000 cuts as I hastened to get out of the place before we were discovered.

Next, the shower —a wonderful long, hot shower to wash out the salt. Once finished, we had only to dress and creep out, then it would be down to the village for some food. I had just switched off the shower and was

reaching for my towel when the outer door opened. I cringed in my cubicle.

Then, the last thing we wanted to hear: a typical Home Counties voice (female).

'Are you sure you're all right Pamela?'

Pamela (gently sobbing), 'Yes, I think so.'

Third Home Counties female,

'Well, I think all men are swine!'

Three showers were hastily switched on again.

And over the next 30 minutes we learned a lot of things about men which we hadn't known before. When the coast was finally clear we were red-faced and wrinkled like prunes. • *Roger Walsh*

'Blind' navigation

There was a reassuring phrase in the introduction to our Yachtmaster examination leaflet: 'All exams are nerve-racking, even for highly experienced or professional skippers, but you can unwind by talking to the examiner and ensuring you make a favourable initial impression.'

We had been offered a Bénéteau 32s5 for our Yachtmaster exam. We set off for four days of man-overboard drills, blind navigation and passage-planning. Arriving in Carrick Roads on the fourth day, we were full of confidence in our abilities, but nervous about the forthcoming exam. We were to meet our examiner on the fuel berth at Falmouth Town Marina.

I had the helm as we motored in, intent on arriving at exactly 1600. The tide was near the bottom of the ebb and I was concentrating on giving clear and concise instructions on mooring to the crew...when our stately progress came to a slow and undignified halt.

Thirty feet off the port bow was a large black post, topped by an easterly cardinal. Thirty feet further on was an awestruck RYA Examiner, clearly searching for hidden cameras or Jeremy Beadle. He grabbed his overnight bag and strode purposefully up the pontoon, obviously bent on returning home with stories of unbelievable sailing incompetence.

Having arrived on this 'obviously uncharted' mudbank, our instructor said loudly—and I quote: 'And now for the second part

PRYTON

of the exercise—heeling the boat to reduce her draught by using crew weight on the boom and motoring off astern.'

Off we slid and, moments later, we were moored neatly on the pontoon, desperately attempting to assume a nonchalant air.

With the Examiner collected, mollified and provided with coffee, the exam commenced...I could not help but notice his almost paranoid interest in my chart work, knowledge of buoyage and proximity to unseen but well-marked mudbanks.

• *M F B Sothcott*

Getting your goat

Crimson Rambler and mud seem to have an irresistible attraction.

I was in the Fiers d'Ars on the Ile de Ré, near La Rochelle. Going up the narrow cut to the town we ran on to some mud on a falling tide. We knew what to do—with only a 4-hp engine, when you were on, you were on until the tide rose. So, the usual steps were taken to heel the boat uphill and we settled down for the rest of the day.

Too late, I discovered that instead of grounding in the main channel, as I had thought, we were in a branch creek and therefore heeling downhill, not uphill. Consequently, the boat soon lay over on her beam ends with the top of the mast overhanging the bank.

There were cows grazing in the field beyond and along the bank and, as cows will, it was not long before one got the idea that I had kindly placed my mast just there and at just the right height for her to scratch her back. This indignity was bad enough, as well as not being very good for my mast, but worse was to follow...The cow was followed by a goat which ate my RCC burgee.

Being a very junior member of the RCC (I was then the youngest member), it was many years before I dared to admit what had happened. • *Hugo du Plessis*

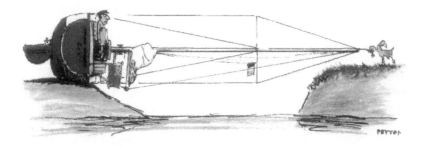

It's a stitch up

As we approached La Belle Ile, off the Brittany coast, we felt we could at last congratulate ourselves on reaching foreign shores. Our voyage from the Isle of Skye towards Gibraltar on a 70-year-old gaff-rigged cutter had provided almost too many notable incidents, but here we were, finally, in French waters with everything going well, looking forward to a night in a harbour, after several at sea. Nearing the island we began to encounter French yachts out for an afternoon jaunt and decided it was time to hoist the French flag. All was in order as we closed the nearest French yacht and gave a companionable wave. Our gestures were not returned with the enthusiasm we had expected, and when the same thing happened with a second boat we began to wonder what we were doing wrong.

Our 50ft wooden boat with tan sails, was usually welcomed with interest, particularly when our Scottish flag was noted. We wondered if we had the courtesy flag incorrectly placed, but no—it was on the starboard crosstree where it should be...there was another British boat with her French flag similarly positioned.

But wait a minute; wasn't there a subtle difference between our French flag and all the others we could now see clearly as we got closer to the harbour entrance. The flag we were flying did, indeed, have the correct red, white and blue stripes, but in the wrong order. A furious flick through the almanac confirmed our suspicions: our flag, which had been with the boat since her time as a fishing boat, announced that we were engaged in pair trawling.

Never had a flag been taken down so quickly, cut from its boltrope, re-stiched and re-hoisted. • *Fiona Mandeville*

Stormy waters

Some years ago, my friend Bob and I joined a yacht on passage from Jersey to France, to gain some sea-time after taking the shore-based RYA Day Skipper course.

At a restaurant in Granville, Bob struck up a conversation with a singlehanded yachtsman who had arrived at the same time as us and who joined our table.

'How do you get time to sail?' asked Bob, explaining that he was a widower with a grown-up family, and that my wife was very understanding.

'I just love sailing,' was the reply. 'In fact, my wife left me because I was always away in the boat.'

'Oh, I am sorry!' exclaimed Bob.

'Yes, I was out one day when a Force 6 suddenly grew into a Force 9 with hardly any warning. By the time I managed to get the main down, I'd lost the jib and had almost been swamped. There was a fair amount of damage to the yacht, but I managed to struggle into the marina. I arrived home well after midnight to find a note from my wife saying that my dinner was in the dustbin, the cat was with her and she'd gone away with my best friend.'

'That's terrible!' said Bob. 'What did you do?'

'I installed roller-reefing. Now I can take in both the main and the jib very quickly now if I need to. It's ideal for singlehanders.'

• *Roger Walsh*

Collision course

In the early 1950s, in New Zealand, I owned an 18ft centreboard yacht called *Wahoo* in partnership with Stacey, the mate of the time. In those days we used to go fishing after work if the weather was suitable. As soon as the five o'clock whistle blew, we would grab a hamburger and some frozen bait, not to mention a crate of refreshment, and rush down to the boat. An hour's motoring with the Seagull outboard would bring us to a good spot in the Rangitoto Channel, and we rarely returned without a good-sized catch in the cockpit.

On this particular trip we were joined by Stacey's neighbour, Dave, a keen fisherman. By nine o'clock, having caught enough, we were headed home. It was one of those very still black nights with no moon but clear visibility. You could see the loom of North Head against the glow of the city lights.

Visitors seem to get a kick out of steering, so we pointed Dave in the right direction and retired to the warmth of the cabin to sip ale and yarn.

Half an hour later, Dave interrupted our reverie, 'Hey chaps, there's two boats coming towards us. Is it OK to go between them?'

We looked at one another vacantly. 'Well how far apart are they Dave?'

'Oh, about 20 yards, I guess.'

'Yeah, she'll be right Dave, go for it mate.'

There was a pause, then, 'One's got a green light and the other's got a red one.' Another pause, then bang!... Our heads collided as Stacey and I both tried to get out of the mainhatch together.

The first to recover grabbed the tiller and slammed it over, while Dave stood wondering what all the panic was about. He soon found out, as a wall of steel slid silently past within spitting distance, leaving us rocking in its wake and listening to the receding thump of the propeller. • *Ted Howe*

Skipper adrift

Winkler, with a crew of beginners, went aground on the Brambles Bank near High Water. Determined to show us how to kedge off, the skipper threw the dinghy over the side and leapt into it with the anchor. The dinghy heeled badly and shipped a lot of water. It wasn't tied on; nor was the kedge. There were no oars either. The sea was choppy. More water was shipped but, as the dinghy and skipper drifted away they grounded in 6in of water.

Lightened by the loss of weight meanwhile, *Winkler* lifted and we motored off fast. But how were we to retrieve the skipper? He had the dinghy, we had the oars. We couldn't get near him without grounding again and it was too far to throw a line.

In the end the skipper solved the problem: he walked out towards us, up to his waist in water, dragging the dinghy and kedge behind. When he was close enough, we threw him a line.

We were much more impressed with the quantity of Scotch he later consumed than with the technique of kedging-off.

• *Ted Osborn*

Express echo

We had been holed up in St Peter Port by the fog that often
seems to come in waves in August. At last came a day when it
lifted enough to see Herm, just, and we decided it was clear
enough, and the tide was right, for a quick escape to Alderney.
There was absolutely no wind so it would just be a quick motor
trip. I boldly assumed that the fog would thicken again only when
the tide turned to flow down-Channel.

We had just cleared north of the Little Russel when plop,
down it came again, thick as ever. It was that very low-lying stuff
that makes you wish you had a crow's nest. The sun was still
shining out of a blue sky.

Bright comments from my daughters suggested that an instant
DIY remote control to the Autohelm from a masthead bosun's
chair would come in handy, but in practice it meant 'on with the
radar' and someone glued to the screen.

We were about half-way to Alderney when, checking on a long-
range view, I saw an echo apparently on a collision course. More
careful study only served to verify the situation so I asked for a 45-
degree turn to starboard. The echo seemed to have a fascination for
us; it was still on a collision course. Another 45 degrees to starboard

and full power, please. It was still on a collision course and by now getting very close. OK, check your lifejackets and the liferaft. In short, accept we are going to be hit hard but try not to panic.

A loud drone accompanied the sight of the bright yellow Islander aeroplane as it flew straight over our mast at only a few hundred feet. It's truly amazing how everyone's sense of time can alter if you do not look at the second hand...that echo must have been doing at least 150 knots. • *Ralph Bowsfield*

Points failure

It was a pleasant mid-week evening as we slipped out of Blyth Marina to return the boat to Amble. A fresh Force 3 directly astern heralded a potential fast trip. But, as often happens in the North Sea, the wind had died within an hour, a light fog surrounded us and we were motoring home.

The fog lifted two hours later, just as we were coming up to Coquet Island. As we slipped between the island and the mainland, the skipper handed me the wheel.

'Just steer for the flashing red light,' he instructed, as he slipped below to put the kettle on. Minutes later his head appeared in the companionway to ask what I was steering for.

'That flashing red light,' I pointed to a light fine on the bow.

'But the entrance is over there!' he replied, pointing to a light flashing to port.

No harm done, but I have not been allowed to forget that a tree branch swaying over a red light on the London to Edinburgh railway line is not 'Fl R' on a chart. • *Brian Dobbs*